Soup, an international cook book

SOUP

an
international
cook book

The Two Continents Publishing Group, Ltd.

Text and Recipes   Annelike Hoogeweegen in cooperation with the International Home Economic
                   Service, Maggi S.A., Kempttal, Switzerland

Adaptation   Irena Chalmers

Photography   Henk van der Heijden with the exception of the photos on pages 29, 32, 36,
              80 and 92, which were supplied by Nestlé Alimentana, Vevey, Switzerland

Photo cover   Ed Suister

Illustrations   Jane Greenwood, London

Lay-out   Joop de Nijs gvn, Castricum

Production   Meijer Pers bv, Amsterdam

Type Setting by   Internationaal Zetcentrum bv, Wormerveer

Printed by   Drukkerij Meijer Wormerveer bv

© 1977 Meijer Pers bv, Amsterdam, The Netherlands

All recipes in this book are intended for 4 persons, unless otherwise mentioned.

Two Continents
30 East 42 Street
New York, New York 10017

Library of Congress Cataloging in Publication Data
Main entry under title:

Soup, an international cook book

   Translation of Soep
   1. Soups I. Hoogeweegen, Annelike
TX757.S6313   641.8'13   76-52782
ISBN 0-8467-0241-X

Printed in The Netherlands

Index

page 7   Introduction

10   Herbs and Spices

12   Stocks

97   Index

98   Index by Ingredients

16   France

23   Switzerland

26   Italy

30   Spain and Portugal

34   Great Britain

40   Belgium

44   Holland

50   Germany

54   Scandinavia

58   Central Europe

63   The Balkan Countries

69   Eastern Europe

73   The Middle East

74   The Far East

81   New Zealand, Australia and Indonesia

83   North America

88   Latin America

93   Africa

Introduction

Soup is one of the oldest dishes known to man and one of the most glorious to waft its way out of the kitchen. Soup is a word that conjures up visions of cauldrons simmering gently for hours over the fire, but it also has sinister connotations with witches, dark brews, magic potions and secret recipes. Happily though, there is no mystery about soup. It is simply water flavored with meat or fish, vegetables or herbs. Apart from these ingredients two other things are needed to make soup: a source of heat and a pan. Once man had discovered the culinary uses of fire, he first used it for roasting meat and it was not long before he devised ingenious ways of preparing soups. The earliest of these was made from water brewed with herbs and was not made in a pot but in hollowed-out sections of tree trunk that were set over glowing coals. Even large stones were pressed into service as saucepans, providing they had an indentation deep enough to hold the liquid. Some tribes in Iran are still using this method of cooking today. The Phoenecians, Egyptians, Persians and Syrians knew very little about soups, but the Greeks and Romans were far more adventurous in the kitchen. It is said the the Emperor Nero drank a huge cup of leek soup every day, not because he liked it but because he had been told that it would strengthen his vocal chords. He was so fond of making speeches that he would go to any length to ensure that he had a fine ringing voice to sway his audience. In Nero's day fresh vegetables, dried pulses and cereals were all frequently used to prepare soups, but soon even this variety was

not enough to please everybody. In the decadent days following the establishment of the Roman Empire, it became a problem to invent new and tasty dishes to set before the jaded palates of guests. It was then rose soup achieved a certain vogue. This soup was not only eaten, but also sprinkled over the body so that the diner would become fragrant inside and out. The recipe included finely ground bird's and pig's brains, fish stock, pepper and wine all mixed with an equal quantity of finely chopped rose leaves...

The original meaning of 'soup' is literally, to feed oneself well. The word comes from the Latin form, 'suppa' which in turn is derived from the two Sanskrit words 'su' and 'po' meaning 'good' and 'to feed oneself'. In France there are two interpretations of the word soup; 'potage' and 'soupe'. A 'potage' is a light soup designed essentially as an appetizer, while 'soupe', being much thicker, is more suitable for a main course.

The days when soups simmered for hours on end are now over, and the venerable broths have given way to commercially prepared canned and packaged soups, dried soups and bouillon cubes. Part of the appeal of these products is that they are ready for use instantly and can be stored easily on the kitchen shelf. In order to give them a personal touch they can be augmented with the addition of a sauce left over from another meal or with extra pieces of meat, chopped vegetables, cream, herbs or a dash of wine or spirits.

There are two methods of making soup depending on whether it is to be a thin clear soup or a thick cream soup. Clear soups are made from either meat or vegetable broths and may be garnished with ingredients such as rice, vermicelli or small pieces of meat or vegetables.

When a starchy food is cooked with the soup it becomes thicker. Thick soups are made from a purée of potatoes, tomatoes, beans, onions, leeks, celery, carrots, cabbage, turnips or other vegetables to which broth or water is added. Soups can be thickened with flour, cornstarch, arrowroot, egg yolks, cream or yogurt.

Though stews often resemble thick soups, they do not fall within the scope of this book. The criteria used for differentiating a soup from a stew is that a stew is eaten with a fork while a soup is eaten with a spoon.

During the last few years there has been an almost passionate yearning to return to the simpler values of our past. Nostalgia has spread a rosy glow over the kitchen and homemade soups have reached new heights of popularity. The language of soup knows no national boundaries for it is loved everywhere from Mongolia to Greenland and from Brazil to the banks of the Volta.

Herbs and Spices

Herbs are the 'tastemakers' of soup and can be used either in the fresh or dried form.

Fresh herbs should not literally be finely chopped, but finely cut, or better still, finely snipped with a pair of scissors.

Dried herbs should be kept in a tightly closed (preferably corked) pot or jar in a cool, dark place. They have a shelf life of about one year and should be discarded after this period.

A *garnishing herb* should be added to the soup just before serving as it will loose much of its flavor and aroma if cooked with the other ingredients in the soup itself.

Spices, unlike garden herbs, usually originate from tropical and sub-tropical areas. They should be used very sparingly because they are quite pungent and produce a 'peppery' effect if used too generously. Spices are sold in dried form, either whole or finely ground. A few well-known spices are cayenne pepper, mace, cinnamon, curry, cloves, mustard, nutmeg, paprika, pepper and saffron.

Basil   The taste and smell of basil is similar to that of bay leaves. Basil can be used in the dried or fresh form in soups containing meat. It is particularly good in lamb soup and also in vegetable soups that contain tomatoes, peas, beans or potatoes.

Bay Leaves   This spice is made from the dried leaves of the bay tree and can be used whole or in the powdered form. The leaves are frequently used in the preparation of stock, and are also suitable for flavoring white or brown bean soups and soups made with leeks, fish or tomatoes as the main ingredients.

Borage (Cucumber Herb)   The leaves should not be cooked in the soup but used as a garnishing herb because the flavor is extremely delicate. The herb, which has sky blue flowers, can be used with dramatic effect as a garnish for vegetable and fish soups.

Caraway (kummel)   Though both leaves and seeds can be used fresh, it is more common to find the seeds dried and sometimes ground. Caraway is excellent with all soups of Central European origin such as mushroom, tomato and sauerkraut soups.

Cayenne Pepper   One cannot be too careful with this spice which is made from Spanish peppers or lomboks. It is used widely in soups that come from the south and especially in bean, tomato and fish soups.

Celery Greens   Ideally celery greens should be used fresh as they lose much of their flavor when dried. The leaves contain large quantities of watersoluble vitamin C and should therefore not be cooked for longer than 15 minutes in the soup or the value of the vitamin will be lost. Whole ribs of celery can be used in preparing stock. The stems have a very pronounced and agreeable flavor.

Chervil   The leaves of the chervil herb have a mild taste of anise and can be used as a garnish for a wide variety of soups. The stems have a more pronounced flavor and can be used in the preparation of vegetable and meat soups. Chervil is excellent with potato and leek soups and can be used as a garnish for soups that have mild and delicate flavors. It is available both in dried and powdered forms.

Chives   Chives should not be cooked in stock or soup because the flavor is lost very rapidly. Chives are used as a garnish for vegetable and cheese soups. The mild taste of onion enhances the flavor of the soup.

Cloves   Cloves are made from the dried buds of the clove tree. They can be used whole or in powdered form in white and brown bean soups.

Curry Curry is a blend of several spices and is always used in powdered form. It is not only used in the preparation of curry soups, but also for chicken and fish soups.

Dill Fresh dill should not be cooked in soup but used as a garnish, particularly for fish soup. It has a slightly sweet flavor and aroma, and in the Scandinavian countries, it is as popular as is parsley in Western Europe.

Garlic Garlic is a bulb that is rather similar to the onion bulb, except that it has 10 or 12 small bulbs contained in an outer skin. These inner bulbs are known as cloves. Garlic is available in fresh, dried and in powdered forms (sometimes with a little salt added). It is recognizable by its pronounced flavor and aroma. In most countries, with perhaps the exception of Great Britain and the Low Countries, it is used generously in the cooking of such soups as tomato, onion, pepper, bean and lentil soups and those prepared with beef, veal and fish stocks.

Lemon balm The leaves of this herb have a delicious fresh taste and smell of lemon. Lemon balm is used as a garnish for mushroom, leek, tomato and fish soups and should always be used sparingly because the flavor can be quite strong. The taste is quickly lost however, and it is not recommended that it be used during the cooking period.

Mace This brown/yellow spice with its very pronounced aroma is made from the dried seed bundle of the nutmeg tree. It is available in leaf, broken or powdered form and is excellent when used as part of the bouquet garni in the preparation of stocks. It is also delicious in bean, vegetable, curry and chicken soups. It should always be used sparingly.

Marjoram Marjoram, with its unusual fragrance, is used in fresh or dried form, in the preparation of vegetable, potato and mushroom soups and in soups made with lamb. It is a sociable herb and is frequently used in conjunction with one or two other herbs.

Mint This is a splended herb for flavoring cucumber, pea and carrot soups and can be used fresh or dried as well as in powdered form.

Nutmeg This spice comes, of course, from the nutmeg tree and is available whole or ground. It should be used with care, but a pinch or two will work miracles in asparagus or cauliflower soups.

Paprika This spice has a beautiful red color and delicious smell. It is made by grinding together different varieties of peppers. It is available in different strengths varying from mild to hot and sweet to sharp. It is particularly good for tomato, oxtail, beef, onion and brown bean soups. It is sometimes sprinkled on the surface of soup and used as a garnish.

Parsley The leaves of this much-loved garden herb should not be cooked for more than 10 minutes in soup because the water soluble A and C vitamins are quickly lost. It can be used as garnish for all except fruit soups. The sprigs, with the stems, may be used in the preparation of soups and stocks. The flavor of the stem is more pronounced that the leaves. Parsley is available in fresh, dried and powdered forms.

Pepper Peppercorns are the fruit of the pepper plant and can be obtained whole (white, black or green), or in the powdered form. It is invaluable in the preparation of nearly every soup. White pepper is more delicate in taste than the black. Green peppercorns are not as pungent as black but have a piquant slightly sweet taste. Freshly ground pepper has infinitely more character than the commercially ground variety.

Rosemary This is a sweet-smelling, powerful herb and can be used fresh, or dried, in soups made with pork, lamb or chicken. It can also be used in fish soups, tomato and mushroom soups to good effect.

Saffron Saffron is made by drying the stamens of certain species of crocus. This spice, usually available in thread form, is very popular in Southern Mediterranean countries where it is used in many different soups. It must always be used with discretion because it can dominate other ingredients.

Savory This is a herb with a particularly interesting flavor and can be used in fresh or dried form, for soups made from beans, peas and lentils, it is also excellent in fish soups, onion and cabbage soups.

Tarragon The leaves of tarragon have a piquant and somewhat mysterious taste that is reminiscent of liquorice, and are at their best when used fresh. It is particularly adaptable for soups prepared with potatoes, fish, chicken and mushrooms. Tarragon can be combined with parsley, chives and chervil and used as a garnishing herb.

Thyme In the fresh, dried or powdered form, this is a delicious herb that complements many soups prepared with meat. It is also good in tomato soup and those made from peas, beans and lentils.

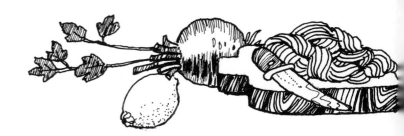

Stocks

Commercial stock preparations are readily available and have become popular because their quality is excellent. They can be bought in a variety of forms. There are beef, chicken and vegetable powders, granules, cubes and broths and they are all excellent for making a stock-based soup.

It cannot be disputed that homemade stocks make the best soups, but today, when ease of preparation is so important, commercial stock bases are widely used even by the most dedicated of cooks. Homemade stock is in itself so delicious that it may even be a shame to use it in a soup that has many other ingredients (and therefore flavors). However, when there is a little homemade stock left over, it can be supplemented with water and a bouillon cube. The recipes in this book leave the choice of homemade or commercial stock to the reader, unless otherwise indicated. Stock in itself has very little food value, but it is excellent for stimulating the appetite: The meat used to make the stock loses its flavor to the cooking liquid, but retains its nutritive value, as the

protein in meat is insoluble in water. With the addition of suitable spices and herbs, the meat can be used in hashes and stews, or used as a garnish for the soup itself.

A stock must simmer for at least 4 hours as the flavors are absorbed slowly by the water. A stock made from bones that have been scraped clean will need to simmer for about 12 hours before all the flavors have been transferred to the cooking liquid.

Pressure Cookers

When stock is made in a pressure cooker the cooking time, which is normally 3–4 hours, is reduced to $1\frac{1}{2}$ hours. Follow the manufacturer's instructions and do not fill the pressure cooker more than half-full with liquid. Stock prepared in a pressure cooker is double strength and can be diluted with water. The only disadvantage is that stock made in this way tends to be rather cloudy.

Light aromatic stocks are made from scraps of veal, lamb and beef. Lean scraps of meat that are free from fat and gristle can still be used after they have been simmered in water, to be incorporated in a stew, meat patties or for making a hash.

Veal stock is milder in flavor than beef stock and is most frequently used as a base for cream soups. If veal bones are used, the stock will become jellied when it is cold. Aromatic stocks are usually made with meat from the shin, or muscular parts of the animal. Marrow bones give a full bodied but fatty stock. The fat can easily be skimmed from the stock after it has cooled. For a smoky flavored nourishing winter soup, use pig's trotters with meat and bone and add a small quantity of bacon.

Chicken and game stocks are made with the carcass and giblets. Do not add the liver or the stock will become cloudy. For a tasty chicken stock, use a boiling chicken and after the stock has been made, use the tender pieces of chicken for a fricassée or chicken croquettes.

Beef Stock

3 pounds beef bones with some meat clinging to the bones
1 pound lean beef scraps
8 cups water
1 teaspoon salt
8 peppercorns
1 bay leaf
1 leek, sliced or
1 additional onion
1 onion, peeled and sliced
1 teaspoon thyme
4 stalks parsley
2 carrots, peeled and sliced
1 blade of mace or
¼ teaspoon nutmeg
strip of lemon peel, optional

At the start of an elaborate dinner, a clear beef consommé is often preferable to a richer cream soup.

Place the bones and beef in a preheated 350° oven and allow to brown for 15 minutes. Place the beef bones, beef and all the remaining ingredients into a large saucepan and bring to the boil slowly in a partially covered pan. Leave to simmer for 4 hours. Do not allow the stock to boil or it will become cloudy.

Strain through a piece of cheesecloth placed inside a colander. Chill the broth for 4 hours and skim off the fat that will rise to the surface. Return to boiling point and season with salt and pepper.

If it is to be served as a clear soup, garnish with parsley or one of the garnishes mentioned under Soup Garnishes.

Simple Beef Stock

½ pound lean beef scraps or
2 pounds beef soup bones with some meat clinging to the bones
6 cups water
1 teaspoon salt
8 peppercorns
1 bay leaf
½ teaspoon thyme
4 stalks parsley
1 carrot, sliced
1 leek, sliced or
1 additional onion
1 onion, peeled and sliced
strip of lemon peel, optional

Scraps of beef can be used to make a light stock, but beef bones are ideal for making a rich full flavored stock. If using bones in the preparation of a simple stock, use those that have some meat clinging to them.

Put all the ingredients into a large saucepan and bring to the boil slowly, skimming the foam as it rises to the surface for the first 10 minutes. Simmer in a partially covered pan for 4 hours. Strain through a piece of cheesecloth placed inside a colander.

Simple Chicken Stock

the carcass of a chicken, preferably raw, but can be roasted or braised
4 cups water
1 teaspoon salt
8 peppercorns
1 bay leaf
1 onion, peeled and sliced
1 teaspoon thyme
4 stalks parsley

Place all the ingredients in a large saucepan and bring to boiling point slowly. Cover and simmer for 3 hours. Strain through a colander. Chill the chicken broth for 4 hours and lift off the fat that will rise to the surface.

Chicken Stock

Chicken stock is made in almost exactly the same way as beef stock. The only difference is that chicken is used instead of beef and the stock is simmered for 3 rather than 4 hours.

Game Stock

2 tablespoons butter
1 onion, peeled and chopped
1 carrot, sliced
6 cups water
1 teaspoon salt
1 bay leaf
1 teaspoon thyme
8 peppercorns
4 stalks parsley
2 cloves
1/8 teaspoon nutmeg
4 juniper berries

Use carcasses and giblets of game birds such as pheasant, duck, turkey or goose, the head, neck and paunch of rabbit or hare or shin of venison.

Cut the game into pieces. Heat the butter in a deep frying pan and fry the game, onion and carrot over low heat for 10 minutes. Add all the remaining ingredients. Cover and simmer for 3 hours. Strain through a colander.

Vegetable Stock

2½ pounds vegetables i.e. onions, carrots, celery, turnip, tomatoes, cauliflower and spinach
2 tablespoons butter
4 stalks parsley
1 teaspoon thyme
¼ teaspoon chervil (optional)
3½ cups water
1 teaspoon salt
freshly ground black pepper

Vegetable stock can be served as a clear soup when it is attractively garnished with chopped parsley or tomato (see soup garnishes). Serve the soup with breadsticks or crackers.
It is a useful stock as a base for a light soup or sauce, and pasta and potatoes are particularly delicious when they are simmered in vegetable stock. Choose only the freshest of vegetables and use a high proportion of mild tasting vegetables, adding only sufficient turnip and spinach to provide a hint of flavor.
Prepare the vegetables and cut them into small pieces. Heat the butter and fry root vegetables for 5 minutes. Add the remaining vegetables and continue frying for 10 minutes. Add ⅓ cup water and let the vegetables 'sweat' for 15 minutes in a covered pan. Add the remaining water and herbs and bring to boiling point. Cover and simmer for 40 minutes. Strain through a colander and season with salt and pepper.

Veal Stock

Veal stock is made in the same way as beef stock. Replace the beef and bones with the equivalent amount of veal bones.

Fish Stock

1½ pounds fish heads, bones and trimmings
4 cups water
1 bay leaf
6 stems parsley
1 tablespoon lemon juice
½ cup dry white wine
4 peppercorns
1 small onion, chopped
1 teaspoon salt

Place all the ingredients in a large saucepan and bring to the boil slowly. Cover and simmer for 30 minutes. Strain through a colander lined with cheesecloth.

TIPS

- Stock deteriorates very quickly, so it is best made in small quantities. Store the stock in the refrigerator in a wide necked jar, so that it does not take up too much space. Fish stock may also be frozen very successfully. Cover the saucepan with a lid or aluminum foil during the cooking time and do not let the liquid boil or the stock will become cloudy. To make a rich brown stock, fry the fish bones in 2 tablespoons of butter until they are golden brown before adding the water.

- Strain the stock after the cooking has been completed. It will then be ready for use for a fish soup, chowder or as the foundation for a fish sauce.

- The simplest and easiest way of removing the accumilated fat from meat or chicken stock is to strain the stock and chill it for at least four hours in the refrigerator. The fat will rise to the surface and harden and it can then be skimmed with a spatula. If time does not permit this chilling period, roll up a piece of absorbent kitchen paper. Hold one end and run the other end slowly over the surface of the stock. The paper will pick up the fat globules. Ice cubes may also be added to lukewarm stock. The fat will congeal around the ice; however, the ice may melt and dilute the stock. Boil it again to reduce it to the original concentration of flavor. If you wish to make stock, but have little time, use lean ground beef to replace the meat scraps and bones. The flavor and aroma from the ground beef will be absorbed by the water in about 30 minutes.

France

According to an old French saying, the only food a soldier needs is soup and salad. And without a doubt, every Frenchman can survive for days on end on this diet, provided, of course, it is accompanied by a glass of wine.

Soups are meant to stimulate the appetite for that which is to follow, and therefore French soups tend to be quite simple, to please the palate and aid the digestion. No self repecting French housewife would end a day's shopping without the ingredients for a *bouquet garni* – that combination of fragrant herbs, which, tied together in a bunch or wrapped in a piece of cheesecloth, find its way into every flavorful soup. The most common staples of this aromatic bouquet are thyme, parsley and bay leaf.

Hearty country soups often make up the main course, as for example the garbure with its morsels of meat and either goose or pork. And no less famous are France's cheese soup, onion soup, Provencal garlic soup, potato and leek soup, not to mention the renowned bouillabaise, a specialty of the coastal region that knows no standard recipe. It simply uses whatever fish is most readily available in a given place and season. The French devotion to food is well known. They not only like to eat, but are ready to talk about the virtues of a dish at the drop of a hat. In 1962 a club of soup eaters – Le Cercle de Gourmets Potagier – was formed, dedicated to restoring the soups of bygone days to their rightful place of honor and to the creation of new ones.

Corsican Tomato Soup

Potato Soup

1 pound potatoes
5 tablespoons butter
2 leeks, thinly sliced, or
1 additional onion
1 onion, finely chopped
4 cups hot water
2 cups milk
2 chicken bouillon cubes
1 teaspoon salt
freshly ground black pepper
2 tablespoons finely chopped parsley

Boil the potatoes in their skins for 20 minutes. Peel and mash the potatoes until smooth. Heat 3 tablespoons of butter and sauté the leeks and onion until soft and translucent. Add the mashed potatoes, water and milk. The soup should be thick and creamy. Add the bouillon cubes and season to taste. Cook gently for another 10 minutes and just before serving swirl in the remaining butter and the parsley.

Corsican Tomato Soup

4 tablespoons butter
8 ripe tomatoes, peeled, seeded and chopped
1½ teaspoons fresh tarragon or
½ teaspoon dried tarragon
1 clove garlic
2 cups water
2 cups milk
1 chicken bouillon cube
1 teaspoon salt
freshly ground black pepper
½ pound ham, finely chopped
1 cup cooked green peas, puréed
2 tablespoons finely chopped parsley

Heat the butter, add the tomatoes, tarragon and garlic. Cover the pan and cook gently for 20 minutes. Discard the garlic. Rub the tomatoes through a strainer, combine with the remaining ingredients and cook gently for 5 minutes until hot.

Pot au Feu Basquaise

4 cups beef stock
3 ripe tomatoes peeled, seeded and chopped
2 small green chili peppers, seeded and cut into small pieces
¼ pound lean ham, diced
1 teaspoon chopped chervil

The basques use the Pot au Feu stock described on page 22 to make this soup, adding tomatoes, chili pepper and ham. Bring the stock to the boil. Add the tomatoes and simmer for 5 minutes. Add the chili peppers and ham and simmer for another 10 minutes. Sprinkle with chervil just before serving.

Leek and Potato Soup

1 pound leeks, thinly sliced
4 cups water or chicken stock
3 tablespoons butter
1 pound potatoes, peeled and diced
1 teaspoon salt
freshly ground black pepper
⅛ teaspoon nutmeg
1 egg yolk
¼ cup milk or light cream
½ cup grated Gruyère or Swiss cheese

Vegetable, leek and potato, and onion soup are, in that order, the most popular soups in France.

Boil the green portion of the leeks in 2 cups of water for 30 minutes. Discard the leeks and reserve the liquid. Heat the butter and add the white part of the leeks, cover and cook gently for 5 minutes. Add the reserved liquid, potatoes, 2 cups of water, salt, pepper and nutmeg. Cover and simmer for another 20 minutes. Rub the soup through a strainer or purée in an electric blender. Stir the egg yolk with the milk and cheese. Add a little of the hot broth, stir and gradually add this mixture to the soup. Heat through but do not boil.

Pot au Feu Basquaise

Artichoke Soup

4 tablespoons butter
4 tablespoon flour
6 cups chicken stock
4 canned or frozen artichoke hearts
1 teaspoon salt
$\frac{1}{8}$ teaspoon nutmeg
2 eggs
$\frac{1}{2}$ cup light cream

Heat the butter, add the flour and cook, stirring constantly until smooth. Gradually add the stock and bring to the boil. Chop 3 of the artichoke hearts and add to the soup together with the remaining whole artichoke heart. Cook gently for 30 minutes. Set aside the whole artichoke heart and rub the soup through a strainer or purée in an electric blender. Chop the reserved artichoke heart and stir it into the soup together with the salt and nutmeg. Stir the eggs with the cream, and stir in a little of the hot soup. Add this mixture to the pot of soup, stirring continuously, but do not allow to come to the boil or the soup will curdle.

Potage Bonne Femme

4 tablespoons butter
1 heart of lettuce finely chopped
1 small cucumber, peeled, seeded and diced
2 sprigs fresh tarragon or
$\frac{1}{2}$ teaspoon dried tarragon
3 sprigs parsley
6 cups chicken stock
$\frac{1}{2}$ teaspoon salt
freshly ground black pepper
$\frac{1}{8}$ teaspoon nutmeg
$\frac{1}{2}$ cup light cream
2 egg yolks, lightly beaten
1 tablespoon chopped parsley

Legend has it that Madame de Pompadour created this soup to captivate Louis xv and strengthen her hold over him.
Heat the butter and sauté the lettuce and a quarter of the cucumber for 3 minutes. Add the tarragon and parsley and cook gently for 5 minutes, Add the stock and the remaining cucumber. Cook gently for 15 minutes until the vegetables are tender. Discard the parsley sprigs. Season with salt, pepper and nutmeg. Combine the cream and lightly beaten egg yolks and add a little of the hot soup. Stir this mixture back into the soup and garnish with parsley.

Garbure Béarnaise

1 cup dried white beans
8 cups water
4 medium sized potatoes, diced
$\frac{1}{2}$ pound fresh green beans
1 teaspoon salt
freshly ground black pepper
$\frac{1}{8}$ teaspoon cayenne pepper
2 cloves garlic, finely chopped
$\frac{1}{2}$ teaspoon marjoram
$\frac{1}{2}$ pound cabbage, finely shredded
$\frac{3}{4}$ pound sliced pickled goose or pork or smoked loin of pork, with 1 tablespoon of goose or pork drippings
8 thin slices of day old brown bread

The natives of the Béarn district, in the foothills of the Pyrenees, claim that a deep, thick-walled, highly glazed pot is a must in the preparation of a good garbure. The unique flavor of this garbure comes from the addition of the pickled goose *(confit d'oie)*. If no goose is available, smoked pork may be substituted. If none of these are at hand, try a ham bone, a hearty garlic sausage or a chunk of lean bacon.
Wash the beans and soak them overnight in the water. Bring them to the boil and cook them gently for about 2 hours. Add the potatoes, green beans, salt, pepper, cayenne, garlic, marjoram and cabbage. Bring the soup back to the boil add the goose or pork and simmer for another 15 minutes. Put the bread into the soup bowls and pour the hot soup over it. The meat and vegetables can also be served separately as a main course and the broth as a first course.

Bouillabaisse

⅔ cup olive oil
2 onions, finely chopped
2 leeks, thinly sliced,
or 1 additional onion
3 cloves garlic, finely chopped
4 ripe tomatoes, peeled, seeded
and chopped
1 strip orange peel
1 bay leaf
⅛ teaspoon saffron
½ teaspoon thyme
4 sprigs parsley
7 celery tops, chopped
water fish
8 cups fish stock
¾ pound eel, cut into 1″ pieces
or substitute any other salt
water fish
1 pound cod fillets cut
into 2″ pieces
½ pound mackerel fillet, cut
into 2″ pieces
½ pound mackerel fillet, cut
into 2″ pieces
½ pound shrimp or 1 squid,
sliced
3 tablespoons finely chopped
parsley
French bread

Of all the methods of preparing this popular fish soup, that of Marseille is without doubt the most renowned. There are countless bouillabaise recipes. Thus, a 19th century version calls for the inclusion of 40 different kinds of fish. Not only do recipes abound, but there are many theories concerning the origins of the name itself. One of these holds that it is derived from the Provençal term *bouillapesce* (fish stock), and another, from the word *bouis* (the end) and *abaisso* (which means to reduce a liquid rapidly by boiling it down). This technique is far more important to the preparation of bouillabaise than the kind of fish that goes into it, for it serves to combine the oil with the stock and prevents it from floating on the top. The choice of fish depends both on availability and individual preference.

Heat the oil in a large saucepan and gently cook the onions, leeks and garlic for 5 minutes. Add the tomatoes, orange peel, bay leaf, saffron, thyme, parsley and celery tops and continue cooking for another 5 minutes.

Meanwhile bring the fish stock to the boil in a separate pan, pour the boiling stock over the vegetables and simmer for 5 minutes. Add the fish and cook for 8 minutes. Add the shrimp and cook for 3 minutes. Put the bread slices into soup bowls, divide the fish among them and pour the soup over the bread and fish. Garnish with parsley.

Garlic Soup
Aïgo-boulido

8 cloves garlic, unpeeled
1 teaspoon salt
freshly ground black pepper
2 cloves
1 bay leaf
½ teaspoon thyme
4 sprigs parsley
3 tablespoons olive oil
4½ cups water
1½ pounds potatoes, diced
⅛ teaspoon saffron
sliced toasted French bread
¼ cup grated Gruyère or
Swiss cheese

According to an old French proverb, boiled garlic keeps a person healthy. Though hot garlic soup undoubtedly has a stimulating effect, its healing potential is not quite so obvious.

Drop the garlic in boiling water for 1 minute. Rinse and peel. Put the garlic into a large saucepan together with the cloves, bay leaf, thyme, parsley and olive oil. Add the water and season to taste. Bring to the boil and simmer for for 30 minutes. Strain the soup and return it to the pan. Add the potatoes and saffron. Simmer for another 20 minutes or until the potatoes are tender. Correct the seasoning and pour over the toasted bread. Sprinkle with grated cheese.

An egg, lightly beaten with a little olive oil, can be added to the soup, or whole eggs can be poached in the broth.

Clear Chicken and Vegetable Broth

Clear Chicken and Vegetable Broth

4 cups stock
1 leek or ½ onion, thinly sliced
2 carrots, finely chopped
4 tablespoons olive oil
8 slices French bread
¼ pound boiled chicken, diced
½ teaspoon salt
freshly ground black pepper

Use the pot au feu stock recipe on page 22 as the base for this soup.
Bring the stock to the boil, add the leek and carrots and cook gently for 10 minutes. Meanwhile heat the olive oil and fry the bread in it until golden brown. Add the chicken to the broth. Season to taste and, when ready to serve, float the toasted bread on top of the broth.

Breton Fish Soup

5 shallots or scallions, finely chopped
4 sprigs sorrel or dill
5 sprigs parsley
4 mint leaves, chopped or ¼ teaspoon dried mint
4 tablespoons butter
1 teaspoon salt
freshly ground black pepper
2½ pounds fish fillets
6 cups water
¼ pound shrimps, shelled
1 cup cooked mussels
½ cup light cream
2 tablespoons finely chopped parsley
2 teaspoons chopped chives

This is a delicious, simple soup from Brittany. It tastes best made with freshly caught fish, but if they are unavailable, substitute frozen fish fillets.
Put all the ingredients except the mussels, shrimp, cream, parsley and chives into a large pan. Bring to the boil and simmer gently for 30 minutes. During the last 5 minutes add the shrimp, mussels and cream. Remove the sprigs of parsley and dill. Sprinkle with the chopped parsley and chives and serve immediately.

Onion Soup

4 tablespoons butter or olive oil
4 large onions, sliced
1 clove garlic, finely chopped
½ teaspoon sugar
1 tablespoon flour
4 cups beef or chicken stock
¾ cup dry white wine, (optional)
1 teaspoon salt
freshly ground black pepper
thick slices day old French bread
¾ cup grated Gruyère or Swiss cheese

Heat the butter and sauté the onions and garlic for 5 minutes. Add the sugar, and flour. Stir and cook gently for 5 minutes. Add the stock and optional wine and maintain at boiling point for 15 minutes. Season to taste. Put the slices of bread into individual earthenware bowls, pour the hot soup over them and sprinkle with the grated cheese. Brown the cheese in a hot oven or under a broiler for 2 minutes. Serve piping hot.

Beef and Vegetable Soup
Pot au Feu

1 pound lean beef
1 beef bone
10 cups water
1 tablespoon salt
12 peppercorns
1 turnip, peeled and quartered
1 large onion, quartered
5 leeks, or 3 onions, sliced
2 tablespoons tomato paste
1 tablespoon lemon juice
1 teaspoon rosemary
2 cloves garlic, halved
3 cloves
3 carrots, diced
4 potatoes, peeled and diced
½ pound green peas
½ pound green beans

This soup traditionally is served as two separate courses : First the stock, accompanied by French bread, followed by the meat and vegetables. However, it can also be eaten as a one-course soup meal.
Put the meat and meat bone into a large pot with the water, salt, peppercorns, turnip, onion, 3 leeks (or substitute onions), tomato paste, lemon juice, rosemary, garlic and cloves. Cover, bring to the boil slowly and skim off the foam as it forms. Simmer for 6 hours very slowly. Chill for 4 hours and carefully lift off the fat that will rise to the surface. Return the beef to the soup, together with the carrots, remaining leeks, potatoes, peas and beans. Simmer for 15 minutes. Slice the beef and serve it and the vegetables separately or with the soup. Serve with French bread, radishes, gherkins and mustard.

Billi-Bi

3 quarts mussels
2 onions, quartered
4 celery tops, chopped
2 cups fish stock
2 cups dry white wine
1 teaspoon salt
freshly ground black pepper
1 cup light cream

This soup is said to have originated either in Paris or Normandy. Some sources claim that it is the creation of Barthe, the chef of the renowned Paris restaurant Maxim's, and named in honor of one of its regular customers named Billy. According to another account, the soup was first made in Sallenelles in Normandy during the 1944 invasion as a farewell meal for an American G.I. by the name of Billy Bye, and later became Billi-Bi, which incidentally also means mussels. Be that as it may, it is a delicious soup.
Wash the mussels under cold running water and scrub them well to remove any sand. Remove the 'beards' from the mussels. Discard any that are open. Put the mussels in a large pan with the onions and celery tops. Cover and cook for 10 minutes. Shake the pan from time to time to distribute the juices evenly. Remove the mussels from the shells and strain the liquor through several thicknesses of cheesecloth. Add the fish stock and wine to the strained mussel liquor. Season to taste and simmer gently for 1 hour. Strain the liquid once more. Add the mussels and cream and correct the seasoning. Serve either hot or well chilled.

Switzerland

The excellent Swiss cuisine is best known for its fondues and soups. Often a whole meal is made from an appetizer followed by a hearty soup and even on more formal occasions, the soup is always an important part of the dinner.

It is often difficult for a tourist to discover the unique Swiss dishes because the food found in restaurants seems to be French, Italian German. However, regional specialties do exist and here are a few favorite soups from Switzerland.

Ticino Vegetable Soup

6 tablespoons butter
1 cucumber, diced
1 leek, thinly sliced, or
1 additional onion
1 celery root, diced or
4 stalks celery, sliced
2 medium sized tomatoes, peeled, seeded and chopped
1 carrot, diced
2 cups cabbage, shredded
1 clove garlic, finely chopped
8 cups water
4 chicken bouillon cubes
$\frac{1}{4}$ cup uncooked rice
3 medium sized potatoes
$\frac{1}{3}$ pound bacon, diced
2 sprigs fresh basil or
$\frac{1}{2}$ teaspoon dried basil
2 tablespoons finely chopped parsley
1 teaspoon salt
freshly ground black pepper
$\frac{1}{2}$ cup grated Parmesan cheese

In Ticino, the Italian canton of Switzerland, this thick soup is usually served as a main course, accompanied by bread and a glass of wine.

Heat the butter and fry the vegetables for 15 minutes over low heat. Add the water and bouillon cubes and simmer, uncovered for 30 minutes. Add the rice, potatoes and bacon and continue cooking gently for another 20 minutes. Stir in the basil and parsley and season with salt and pepper. Serve the cheese separately.

Aargau Spinach Soup

2 tablespoons butter
2 onions, finely chopped
$\frac{2}{3}$ cup bacon, diced
2 tablespoons flour
$\frac{1}{2}$ cup milk
4 cups chicken stock
$\frac{1}{2}$ cup spinach, chopped, plus a few small whole leaves
$\frac{1}{4}$ teaspoon nutmeg
1 teaspoon salt
freshly ground black pepper
2 tablespoons light cream
$\frac{1}{4}$ cup grated Parmesan cheese
1 cup croutons

Heat the butter and sauté the onions for 3 minutes. Add and sauté the bacon for 3 minutes. Stir in the flour and add the milk and stock gradually. Add the chopped spinach, nutmeg, salt and pepper and simmer gently for 10 minutes. Stir the cream with the grated cheese and add to the soup just before serving. Garnish with the whole spinach leaves and croutons.

Geneva Potato Soup

6 cups beef stock
4 medium sized potatoes, diced
$\frac{1}{2}$ teaspoon thyme
2 carrots, sliced
2 stalks celery, sliced
1 leek or onion, finely chopped
3 egg yolks
1 cup light cream
1 teaspoon salt
freshly ground black pepper
$\frac{1}{8}$ teaspoon nutmeg
2 tablespoons finely chopped chives or parsley

Bring the stock to boiling point. Add the potatoes, thyme and vegetables. Cover and simmer for 30 minutes. Rub the soup through a strainer or purée in an electric blender. Stir the egg yolks with the cream, add a few spoonfuls of the hot broth and return the mixture to the soup. Heat through but do not allow to boil or the soup will curdle.

Season with salt and pepper. Add the nutmeg and garnish with the chopped chives.

Cabbage Soup

3 tablespoons butter
6 cups cabbage, shredded
1 tablespoon brown sugar
3 tablespoons flour
4 cups chicken stock
freshly ground black pepper
1 teaspoon salt
1 cup milk
⅓ cup lean bacon, diced and cooked
¼ pound salami or other diced sausage

Heat the butter and sauté the cabbage for about 5 minutes. Stir in the sugar. Add the flour and stir in the stock gradually. Cover and simmer over low heat for 30 minutes. Season with salt and pepper. Just before serving, stir in the milk. Add the bacon and salami and heat until hot.

Jura Mountain Soup

4 tablespoons butter
2 cups chopped mushrooms
1 onion, finely chopped
2 medium sized potatoes, diced
1 teaspoon salt
freshly ground black pepper
¼ teaspoon ground cloves
dash Tabasco sauce
¼ teaspoon thyme
4 cups milk
2 egg yolks
½ cup grated Gruyère cheese
sliced French bread, toasted

Heat the butter and sauté the mushrooms and onion for 5 minutes. Add the potatoes and cook gently in the butter for 12 minutes. Season with salt and pepper and add the ground cloves, Tabasco sauce and thyme. Add the milk. Stir the egg yolks with the grated cheese and stir in a little of the hot broth. Return the mixture to the soup, stirring continuously. Heat through but do not boil. Correct the seasoning and serve with toasted French bread.

Pigeon Soup

the carcass and giblets of 3 roasted pigeons
6 cups chicken stock
1 leek or onion, thinly sliced
1 cup sliced mushrooms
2 stalks celery, thinly sliced
1 bay leaf
1 teaspoon salt
⅛ teaspoon nutmeg
3 juniper berries
2 sprigs fresh thyme or 1 teaspoon dried thyme
1 tablespoon cornstarch dissolved in
¼ cup port wine
2 slices day-old bread
¼ cup milk
1 egg
1 tablespoon breadcrumbs
1 cup roasted pigeon meat, ground

Put the carcass and giblets into a large saucepan with the chicken stock, leek or onion, mushrooms, celery, bay leaf, salt, nutmeg, juniper berries and half of the thyme. Cover and simmer gently for 2 hours. Strain the stock. Stir the cornstarch into the port. Return the soup to simmering point and add the cornstarch mixture. Soak the bread in the milk. Squeeze dry and add the egg, breadcrumbs and ground pigeon meat. Shape the mixture into small balls and poach in the simmering broth for 5 minutes.

Jura Mountain Soup

Cabbage Sou

24

Italy

In the days of the Roman Empire it was a great status symbol to be able to employ a Greek cook. Greek cooks commanded huge sums at the slave markets and the Roman cuisine blossomed under their hands. When Catherine de Medici left Venice to marry the Duke of Orléans, the future King Henry II of France, her entourage included an army of cooks and pastry chefs. Legend claims that it was Catherine's staff who taught the French how to cook and laid the foundation for the French cuisine as we know it today.

The typical Italian soup is a happy blend of vegetables and meat or fish enhanced by a whiff of garlic, herbs and Parmesan cheese.

Minestra is the Italian word for vegetable soup and minestrone is the name of the popular thick vegetable, pasta and bean soup. Although in recent years, the Italians have become increasingly diet-conscious, they have not yet cut down on their glorious pasta-filled soups.

Parsley and Rice Soup

2 tablespoons olive oil
2 onions, chopped
4 medium sized potatoes, grated
5 cups chicken stock
4 tablespoons finely chopped parsley
⅓ cup uncooked rice
1 teaspoon salt
freshly ground black pepper
2 tablespoon butter
⅓ cup grated Parmesan or other hard cheese

Heat the oil and sauté the onions for 5 minutes until golden brown. Add the potatoes, chicken stock and half of the parsley. Bring to boiling point and stir in the rice. Cover and simmer for 20 minutes until the rice is soft and fluffy. Season with salt and pepper. Just before serving, stir in the butter, cheese and remaining parsley.

Macaroni and Bean Soup
Pasta e fagioli

¾ pound white beans, or lentils or brown beans
8 cups water
1 tablespoon olive oil
4 slices bacon, diced
1 onion, finely chopped
2 cloves garlic, finely chopped
1 teaspoon rosemary
1 thick slice celery root diced or
2 stalks celery sliced
2 teaspoons tomato paste
⅓ teaspoon salt
freshly ground black pepper
½ pound elbow macaroni
2 tablespoons finely chopped summer savory

Wash the beans and soak them overnight in the water. Simmer gently for 2 hours, until the beans are tender. Rub half of the cooked beans through a strainer or purée in an electric blender and return to the pan. Heat the oil and sauté the bacon, onion, garlic, rosemary and celery for about 5 minutes. Add the beans and soup. Add the tomato paste and season with salt and pepper. Add the macaroni and sprinkle with chopped savory.

This soup can be served as a main course, accompanied by French bread and a salad.

Cream of Celery Soup

4 tablespoons butter
5 cups sliced celery
2 carrots, sliced
1 leek or 1 small onion, sliced
5 cups chicken stock
1 teaspoon salt
freshly ground black pepper
1 egg yolk
½ cup light cream
2 tablespoons Parmesan cheese

Heat the butter and sauté the celery, carrots and leek or onion for 5 minutes. Add 2 cups of the chicken stock and simmer for 20 minutes until the vegetable are tender. Rub through a strainer or purée in an electric blender. Return to the heat, add the remaining chicken stock and season with salt and pepper. Return to boiling point. Stir the egg yolk with the cream and grated cheese and add a few spoonfuls of the hot broth. Reduce the heat under the soup and stir in the egg mixture. Do not allow the soup to regain the boil or the egg yolk will curdle.

Fish Soup

¼ cup olive oil
1 onion, finely chopped
1 cup celery tops, finely chopped
3 cloves garlic, finely chopped
3 sprigs fresh thyme or
½ teaspoon dried thyme
1 teaspoon chili powder
2 tablespoons flour
6 tomatoes, peeled, seeded and chopped
½ cup dry white wine
1½ cups fish stock
2 pounds assorted fish and shellfish such as cod, turbot, cooked shrimp and mussels cut into bite sized pieces
1 teaspoon salt
freshly ground black pepper
2 tablespoons finely chopped parsley
grated rind 1 lemon
12 slices French bread, toasted

The pungent rich sauce which forms the base of this soup can be prepared in advance and reheated. The flavor of the soup will depend on the type and variety of the fish used.

Heat the oil and sauté the chopped onion until golden brown. Stir in the celery tops, garlic, thyme, chili and flour. Cook for 2 minutes and add the tomatoes. Simmer gently for 4 minutes. Add the wine and simmer for another 20 minutes. Stir in the fish stock and cook for 5 minutes.

If prepared in advance up to this point, reheat the sauce, add the fish and cook for 8 minutes. Season with salt and pepper and sprinkle with the parsley and grated lemon rind. Put 3 slices of the toasted bread into individual serving bowls and spoon the soup and fish over them.

Eggplant Soup

3 tablespoons olive oil
1 medium sized eggplant, cut into 1″ cubes
1 teaspoon salt
freshly ground black pepper
5 cups chicken stock
2 tablespoons tomato paste
1 tablespoon butter
1 tomato, peeled, seeded and chopped
1 cup cooked green peas
2 tablespoons finely chopped parsley

Heat the olive oil until very hot and sauté the eggplant cubes for 5 minutes. Season with salt and pepper. Stir in the stock and tomato paste. Bring to boiling point, reduce the heat and simmer for 10 minutes. Rub through a strainer or purée in an electric blender. Strain the soup and return to a clean saucepan. Reheat and swirl in the butter. Just before serving, stir in the tomato, peas and parsley.

Creamed Ham Soup

½ pound boiled ham, ground
½ cup heavy cream
2 tablespoons grated Parmesan cheese
5 cups hot chicken stock
2 eggs, lightly beaten
1 cup croutons

Combine the ham, cream, cheese and one cup of the stock in the top of a double boiler. Add the eggs and stir continuously until the mixture is smooth and creamy. Add the remaining stock, stirring constantly but do not allow to boil. Serve the soup garnished with croutons.

Chestnut Soup

2 tablespoons oil
¼ cup mushrooms, diced
1 onion, chopped
2 tablespoons tomato paste
4 cups chicken stock
4 cups milk
1 (8 ounce) can unsweetened chestnut purée
½ small apple, grated
½ cup heavy cream
2 tablespoons finely chopped celery tops or parsley

Heat the oil and sauté the mushrooms and onion for 3 minutes. Add the tomato paste and chicken stock. Add the milk and stir in the chestnut purée. Simmer gently for 10 minutes. Just before serving stir in the apple, cream and celery tops or parsley.

Chestnut Soup

Genoese Minestrone

2 tablespoons olive oil
2 carrots, diced
2 onions, chopped
2 leeks, or 1 additional onion, chopped
3 potatoes, peeled and diced
¼ pound spinach, chopped
5 cups chicken stock
½ pound cooked white beans
1 teaspoon salt
freshly ground black pepper
2 cloves garlic, finely chopped
1 tablespoon finely chopped fresh basil or 1 teaspoon dried basil
2 tablespoons finely chopped parsley
4 slices bacon, diced
¼ pound macaroni
½ cup grated Parmesan cheese

Minestrone is one of the great Italian classics. Every region has its own recipe, but all of them have 3 ingredients in common; vegetables, beans and pasta, and all minestrones are thick soups. This Genoese minestrone was created by the famous Italian chef Romeo Salta. New York City has a restaurant named for him and it is considered one of the world's great eating places.
Heat the oil, sauté the carrots, onions, leeks, potatoes and spinach for 5 minutes. Add the chicken stock and beans and season with salt and pepper. Bring to boiling point, reduce the heat and simmer gently for 20 minutes. Make a paste from the garlic, basil, parsley and bacon, (this can be done in advance), and add this to the soup together with the macaroni. Simmer for about 15 minutes. Sprinkle the cheese on the soup or serve in a separate bowl.

Maritata Soup

5 cups beef or chicken stock
1 cup thin noodles
4 tablespoons butter, softened
¾ cup grated Parmesan cheese
4 egg yolks
1 cup heavy cream

Maritata is the Italian word for 'married' and this soup is indeed a happy union of fragrant stock, cheese, butter, eggs and cream. It can be served as a main course, accompanied by French bread and a salad.
Heat the stock, add the noodles and cook for 5–8 minutes. Beat together the butter, cheese and egg yolks and add the cream gradually. Add a few spoonfuls of the hot stock, stirring constantly. Add this mixture to the hot soup and serve immediately.

Minestrone Ernesto

¼ pound white or brown beans
or lentils
10 cups water
¼ pound lean bacon, diced
½ small head cabbage, shredded
½ pound green beans, chopped
¼ pound green peas
3 stalks celery, sliced
2 small zucchini or 1 cucumber,
sliced thickly
3 small potatoes, peeled and
diced
1 teaspoon marjoram
1½ teaspoon salt
¼ cup macaroni
7 tablespoons grated Parmesan
cheese
8 walnuts, chopped
6 anchovy fillets
4 tablespoons olive oil

Wash the beans and soak them overnight in the water. Bring them to the boil and simmer for 2 hours. Add the bacon, vegetables, potatoes, marjoram and salt. Cover and simmer for 30 minutes until the vegetables are tender. Ten minutes before serving add the macaroni. Mix the cheese with the nuts and anchovies using a pestle and mortar or an electric blender. Add the olive oil into the mixture gradually. Form this mixture into small balls and poach in the hot soup for 5 minutes.

Minestrone Ernesto

Clear Soup with Poached Eggs

5 cups chicken stock
4 eggs
½ cup grated Parmesan cheese
4 slices French bread, toasted

Bring the stock to boiling point. Reduce the heat and simmer gently for 5 minutes. Poach the eggs in the simmering stock by breaking each into a cup and slipping them one by one into the stock. Simmer the eggs for 4 minutes until the whites are firm but not hard. Remove them from the soup with a slotted spoon and place each in a soup bowl. Cover the eggs with hot stock. Place a generous spoonful of cheese on each slice of toast and float it on top of the soup. Serve any remaining cheese separately.

Stracciatella

2 eggs, lightly beaten
3 tablespoons Parmesan
cheese, grated
2 tablespoons breadcrumbs
½ teaspoon salt
⅛ teaspoon nutmeg
5 cups chicken stock
2 tablespoons finely chopped
parsley

Mix the eggs, cheese, breadcrumbs, salt and nutmeg until smooth and stir in ½ cup of the stock. Bring the remaining stock to boiling point. Reduce the heat and add the egg mixture, stirring constantly. Cook for 3 minutes continuing to stir until the eggs take on the appearance of tiny flakes. Garnish with parsley and serve immediately.

Spain and Portugal

The very first cook book ever to be published was a 1477 edition of the *Libre de Coch*. (The Cook's Book). The fact that the book was written and published in Spain is very surprising because even today there are very few cook books in either Spain or Portugal and most recipes are handed down from mother to daughter by word of mouth.

The cooking of Spain and Portual is very similar and has remained essentially unchanged for hundreds of years. The most famous soup in Spain is, of course, Gazpacho. This is a cold vegetable soup and can be made in a variety of ways. If you were to ask a Spaniard for the recipe, the directions would be very simple. All you need do, he would say, would be to take a handful of vegetables and herbs, chop them up together and let them sit for a while... and that is all there is to it. Some people think that the Portuguese cooking is slightly more elaborate than the Spanish, but this may apply only to the soups. There are two hundred recipes for one of the favorite soups in Portugal. All are based on one simple ingredient; dried fish. The recipe follows...

Spanish Egg Soup

6 cups chicken stock
4 egg yolks
juice 1 lemon
¼ pound cooked chicken, diced
1 teaspoon salt
freshly ground black pepper
1 cup croutons

Bring the stock to boiling point. Beat the egg yolks until light and fluffy and combine with the lemon juice. Add a little of the hot stock and stir into the stock in the saucepan. Do not reboil. Garnish with the cooked chicken. Season with salt and pepper and serve with croutons.

Gazpacho

4 large ripe tomatoes, peeled, seeded and diced
½ cucumber, peeled and diced
2 shallots or 4 scallions, finely chopped
1 green pepper, seeded and
2 cloves garlic, finely chopped
2 tablespoons finely chopped parsley
¼ cup olive oil
2 tablespoons lemon juice
1 teaspoon salt
freshly ground black pepper
⅛ teaspoon cayenne pepper
4 cups chicken broth, iced
8 ice cubes
fried croutons

Gazpacho is a regional specialty of Andalusia, a particularly warm part of Spain. Served ice cold, it can best be described as a salad in liquid form. There are numerous varieties of this popular cold soup, but three ingredients are common to all of them : tomatoes, garlic and olive oil. The other components may very according to personal taste or local conditions, but there can be no Gazpacho without these three.

The following recipe is easy to prepare and can be varied by the addition of onions, hard-boiled eggs, olives, tomato juice or any other compatible ingredient. Combine the tomatoes, cucumber, shallots or scallions, garlic, and green pepper in a bowl. Add the parsley, olive oil, lemon juice, salt and pepper, cayenne and chicken broth. Stir, cover and chill for 4 hours. Place 2 ice cubes in each soup bowl and pour in the soup. Serve with croutons fried in butter.

Carmen's Chestnut Soup

1 pound chestnuts, cooked and peeled
⅓ cup bacon, diced
3 onions, roughly chopped
1 carrot, cut into 1″ pieces
1 teaspoon salt
freshly ground black pepper
¼ teaspoon nutmeg
5 cups beef or veal stock
1 teaspoon brown sugar
¼ cup light cream
2 tablespoons finely chopped parsley

To peel the chestnuts, score them deeply and boil for 30 minutes. In a saucepan, combine the peeled chestnuts with the bacon, onion, carrot, salt and pepper. Add the nutmeg. Add half of the stock and simmer for 30 minutes. Set aside a few of the chestnuts. Rub the soup through a strainer or purée in an electric blender. Add the remaining stock and heat until hot. Just before serving, stir in the brown sugar, cream and parsley. Chop the remaining chestnuts and use them to garnish the soup.

Portuguese Green Soup

4 cups water
2 tablespoons olive oil
2 potatoes, peeled and sliced
2 chicken bouillon cubes
5 cabbage leaves, shredded
⅛ teaspoon nutmeg

Bring the water to boiling point and add the olive oil, pouring in a thin stream. Add the potatoes and bouillon cubes. Simmer the soup for 15 minutes until the potatoes are soft. Mash the potatoes, or rub the soup through a strainer or purée in an electric blender. Return the soup to boiling point. Add the cabbage and simmer for 15 minutes. Sprinkle with nutmeg just before serving.

Spanish Vegetable Soup
Potage Boronia

⅓ cup olive oil
1 medium sized eggplant, cut into 1″ cubes
½ pound Spanish melon diced
3 medium sized tomatoes, peeled, seeded and chopped
2 onions, finely chopped
1 clove garlic, finely chopped
⅛ teaspoon cayenne pepper
¼ teaspoon saffron
1 teaspoon sugar
4 cups chicken stock
3 slices toasted bread, crumbled
1 teaspoon salt
4 eggs poached

Heat the oil in a large frying pan. Sauté the eggplant over high heat for 5 minutes. Add and sauté the melon and the remaining vegetables for 5 minutes. Stir in the cayenne pepper, saffron and sugar and cook gently for 10 minutes. Rub through a strainer or purée in an electric blender. Stir in the hot stock and crumbled toast. Season with salt and simmer gently while preparing the eggs. To poach the eggs, bring 4 cups of water with 1 teaspoon salt and 1 teaspoon vinegar to boiling point. Break each egg into a saucer and slip it into the boiling water. Simmer for 4 minutes until the white is firm but the yolk is still soft. Lift the egg out of the water with a slotted spoon, place in a soup bowl and add the soup.

Spanish Bean Soup

½ pound brown beans
4 cups water
4 cloves
4 bay leaves
½ cup celery tops, chopped
1 large onion, chopped
1 clove garlic, finely chopped
1 tablespoon olive oil
¼ teaspoon dry mustard
⅛ teaspoon cayenne pepper
dash Tabasco sauce
2 tablespoons sherry
½ cup sour cream
½ lemon, very thinly sliced
1 hard-boiled egg, finely chopped

Wash the beans and soak them overnight in the water. Add the cloves, bay leaves and celery tops. Cover and cook over low heat for 1 hour. Sauté the onion and garlic in the hot oil. Stir in the mustard, cayenne pepper and Tabasco sauce. Add this mixture to the soup and simmer for another 30 minutes. Add the sherry. Garnish with the sour cream, sliced lemon and chopped egg.

Portuguese Fish Soup
Caldeirada

2 cups fish stock
1 cup port wine, or 1 additional cup of stock
2 tablespoons olive oil
1 onion, finely chopped
1 clove garlic, finely chopped
2 tablespoons tomato paste
½ teaspoon salt
freshly ground black pepper
2 pounds assorted fish, such as dried cod soaked for 12 hours, fresh cod, haddock or sea trout, cut into bite-sized pieces
¼ pound cooked shrimp or mussels

This soup is often served with French bread as a main course.
Bring the stock to boiling point and stir in the port. Heat the olive oil and sauté the chopped onion and garlic for 5 minutes. Stir in the tomato paste and season with salt and pepper. Pour in the hot stock and return to boiling point. Add the fish and cook gently for 5 minutes. Add the shrimp or mussels. Serve with fresh or toasted French bread.

Spanish Asparagus and Hazelnut Soup

2 tablespoons butter
¾ cups shelled hazelnuts
(filberts), finely chopped
1 onion, finely chopped
½ pound diced ham
5 cups chicken stock
¼ cup dry sherry
1 teaspoon salt
freshly ground black pepper
1½ cups cooked or canned
asparagus, well drained and cut
into 2″ lengths
½ cup light cream

The combination of asparagus and hazelnuts may seem rather unusual, but together they make a delicious soup. Heat the butter and sauté the nuts for 5 minutes until golden brown. Sauté the onion in the same butter for 3 minutes until softened. Add the ham. Stir in the chicken stock and add the sherry. Season with salt and pepper. Simmer the soup for 15 minutes. Add the asparagus and heat until hot. Stir in the cream just before serving.

Spanish Chick Pea Soup

½ pound dried chick peas
10 cups water
¼ pound bacon, diced
2 ounces uncooked ham
1 pound uncooked chicken
½ pound uncooked lean beef
1 soup bone
1½ teaspoons salt
4 medium sized potatoes,
peeled and diced
2 onions, finely chopped
2 cloves garlic, finely chopped
4 carrots, cut into 1″ lengths
1 head Boston lettuce, shredded
2 leeks, or 1 onion, thinly sliced
1 teaspoon oregano
½ teaspoon caraway seeds

This thick chick pea soup is often served as a main course. It is related to the South American Olla Podrida (literally, fragrant pot) and puchero soups. The many variations of this soup are a reflection of its great popularity.
Wash the chick peas and soak them overnight in the water. Bring them to the boil, simmer for 30 minutes and add the bacon, ham, chicken, beef, soup bone, and salt. Simmer gently for 1½ hours skimming occasionally to remove any foam that rises to the surface. Add the potatoes, vegetables, oregano and caraway seeds. Simmer for another 30 minutes. Strain the broth and slice the meats and vegetables. Arrange on a hot platter and serve the clear broth separately.

Spanish Asparagus and Hazelnut Soup

Spanish Garlic Soup

¼ cup olive oil
10 cloves garlic, finely chopped
4 cups chicken stock
1 cup dry sherry
1 teaspoon salt
freshly ground black pepper
8 slices French bread
1 cup grated Parmesan or other
hard cheese

Heat the oil and sauté the garlic for 3 minutes until lightly browned. Bring the stock and sherry to boiling point. Add the oil and garlic and season with salt and pepper. Simmer the soup for 30 minutes, strain and return to the heat.
Sprinkle the sliced bread with the grated cheese and put under a broiler or in a hot oven for 3 minutes. Arrange the slices in soup bowls and pour the hot soup over them.

Spanish Chick Pea Soup

Royal Soup

2 hard-boiled eggs, chopped
3 slices cooked breast of
chicken, chopped
3 slices cooked ham, chopped
3 slices cooked beef, chopped
8 cups beef stock
1 cup dry sherry
4 sprigs parsley or watercress

Despite its imposing name, this soup is
made from leftover chicken, ham and
beef. It makes an ideal warm weather
main course for it is light yet nourishing
and satisfying.
Heat the eggs, chicken, ham and beef
slowly with the stock and sherry. The
soup is ready to serve as soon as it comes
to the boil. Garnish with parsley or
watercress and serve accompanied by
French bread and a salad.

Portuguese Egg and Tomato Soup

2 tablespoons olive oil
1 large onion, sliced
6 medium sized tomatoes,
peeled,
seeded and chopped
4 cups chicken stock
2 sprigs parsley
$\frac{1}{2}$ teaspoon thyme
1 teaspoon salt
freshly ground black pepper
$\frac{1}{2}$ teaspoon sugar
1 teaspoon butter
2 tablespoons finely chopped
parsley
2 hard-boiled eggs, finely
chopped

Heat the oil and sauté the onion and
tomatoes gently for 10 minutes, stirring
occasionally and pressing down on the
tomatoes to release the juice. Add the
chicken stock, parsley and thyme.
Simmer gently for 30 minutes. Strain and
season with salt and pepper. Add the
sugar. Return to the heat and just before
serving, swirl in the butter. Garnish with
the chopped parsley and hard-boiled
eggs.

33

Lady Curzon Soup

2 egg yolks
½ cup light cream
2 (10½ ounce) cans turtle soup
2 tablespoons slivered almonds
2 tablespoons butter
1 tablespoon curry powder
2 tablespoons dry sherry
½ cup whipped cream

Stir the egg yolks with the light cream. Heat the turtle soup until hot. Stir in the egg and cream mixture and add the almonds. Do not let the soup come to boiling point. Heat the butter, add the curry powder and cook gently for 2 minutes. Add the sherry and add to the hot soup. Serve in soup cups and garnish with a spoonful of whipped cream.

Great Britain

Except for breakfast, British cooking does not enjoy a particularly exalted reputation. Breakfast in a British hotel, however, can be an awesome affair consisting of hot or cold cereal; bacon; eggs, tomatoes; broiled kidneys; smoked haddock; grilled kippers; buttered toast; marmalade; tea or coffee. That should be enough to start the day off well! British soups are also excellent, particularly those made at home. Because of the great influx of immigrants, foreign food is gradually gaining acceptance in Britain and Indian, Greek, Chinese, Vietnamese and the restaurants of many other countries are to be found not only in London but in many of the cities throughout the country.

Chrysanthemum Soup

4 cups chicken stock
2 tablespoons dry sherry
½ teaspoon soy sauce
½ cup young tender spinach leaves, chopped
the petals of 1 large white or yellow chrysanthemum

In Elizabethan times, flowers were commonly used in many recipes and primroses, roses, violets and other flowers were added to flavor hot drinks. Many of these old recipes have recently been revived and add an interesting touch to a meal.

Bring the stock to the boiling point and add the sherry, soy sauce and chopped spinach leaves. Cover and simmer for 5 minutes. To serve, float the petals on top of the soup.

Irish Cabbage Soup

3 medium sized potatoes, peeled and diced
1 onion, chopped
1 carrot, sliced
6 cups cabbage, shredded
6 cups boiling water
6 chicken bouillon cubes
1 teaspoon rosemary
1 bay leaf
1 teaspoon salt
freshly ground black pepper
1 cup light cream

This soup can be prepared well in advance and served as a main course, accompanied by bread and ham or cheese.
Add the vegetables to the boiling water. Add the bouillon cubes, rosemary and bay leaf. Bring back to boiling point. Reduce the heat. Cover and simmer for 20 minutes until the vegetables are tender. Season with salt and pepper. Stir in the cream just before serving and heat until hot.

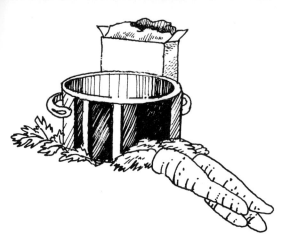

Cock-a-Leekie Soup

4 pound boiling chicken with
the giblets
10 leeks, green and white part
chopped
8 cups water
6 chicken bouillon cubes
1 teaspoon thyme
1 bay leaf
12 prunes soaked in hot tea for
12 hours and drained
1 teaspoon salt
freshly ground black pepper

Prunes are a traditional ingredient of this Scottish specialty, though some Scots substitute ⅓ cup of cream and extra seasonings to replace them.

Put the chicken and giblets into a large saucepan. Add the leeks, water, bouillon cubes, thyme and bay leaf. Bring to boiling point. Reduce the heat, cover and simmer for 3 hours. During the final 30 minutes add the prunes. Remove the chicken. Discard the skin and bones and cut the meat into small pieces. Return the chicken meat to the hot soup and season with salt and pepper.

Cream of Onion Soup

4 tablespoons butter
4 large onions, finely chopped
2 tablespoons flour
3 cups hot water
3 chicken bouillon cubes
2 cups milk
½ teaspoon salt
freshly ground black pepper

Heat the butter and sauté the chopped onions for 5 minutes until golden brown. Stir in the flour and add the hot water and bouillon cubes. Simmer for 20 minutes. Stir in the milk and heat until hot, but do not boil. Season with salt and pepper.

Creamed Crab Soup
Partan Bree

⅓ cup uncooked rice
2 cups milk
1 cup light cream
1 cup chicken stock
14 ounces crab meat
1 tablespoon anchovy paste
½ teaspoon salt if necessary
freshly ground pepper
2 tablespoons finely chopped
parsley

Simmer the rice in the milk for 20 minutes until soft and fluffy. Rub through a strainer or purée in an electric blender. Return to the saucepan and add the remaining ingredients. Season with salt and pepper. Heat until hot and serve in small bowls. Garnish each bowl with parsley.

Hodge Podge

1 pound mutton or lamb, cut
into small pieces
¼ cup flour
2 tablespoons butter
1 tablespoon oil
1 onion, finely chopped
2 carrots, sliced
¾ cup diced turnip
2 cups shredded cabbage
2 teaspoons tomato paste
¼ cup presoaked barley
5 cups boiling water
4 beef bouillon cubes
1 teaspoon salt
freshly ground black pepper
2 tablespoons finely chopped
parsley

Dredge the meat in flour. Heat the butter and oil and brown the meat over high heat. Add the vegetables. Stir in the tomato paste and barley. Add the boiling water and bouillon cubes. Cover and simmer for 1½ hours. Season with salt and pepper and garnish with parsley.

Oxtail Soup

3 tablespoons butter
2 tablespoons oil
1 oxtail cut into sections
5 cabbage leaves, shredded
2 onions, finely chopped
5 cups water
4 beef bouillon cubes
1 bay leaf
1 teaspoon basil
10 peppercorns
2 cloves
$\frac{1}{2}$ teaspoon salt
$\frac{1}{3}$ cup brandy (optional)
5 slices bread, trimmed, diced and fried in butter until crisp croutons are formed

Heat the butter and oil and fry the oxtail until lightly browned. Add the vegetables, water, bouillon cubes, herbs and salt. Cover and simmer for 2 hours. Add more water if necessary. Strain the soup. Cool and skim off any fat that has risen to the surface. Remove the oxtail and cut the meat into small pieces. Heat the soup until hot. Add the oxtail meat and stir in the cognac. Add the croutons just before serving.

Clear Celery Soup

6 stalks celery with the tops, cut into 1″ pieces
5 cups chicken stock
$\frac{1}{4}$ cup heavy cream
2 tablespoons finely chopped parsley

Cook the celery and tops in the chicken stock for 20 minutes. Strain the broth. Just before serving stir a little of the broth into the cream and pour this mixture back into the remaining broth. Heat until hot. Garnish with chopped parsley.

Kidney Soup

3 tablespoons butter
1 onion, finely chopped
$\frac{1}{2}$ pound calf's or lamb's kidney, sliced
1 tablespoon paprika
5 cups water
3 chicken bouillon cubes
grated rind 1 lemon
1 $\frac{1}{2}$ tablespoons flour

This is a much loved soup in the north of England.

Heat the butter and sauté the onion for 3 minutes. Fry the sliced kidney in the same butter together with the paprika. Add 3 cups of water and the bouillon cubes. Add the grated lemon rind. Cover and simmer for 45 minutes. Strain the soup and reserve the kidneys. Stir the flour into the remaining 2 cups of water and add to the hot soup. Cook gently for another 5 minutes, stirring constantly until the soup is thick and smooth. Add the chopped kidneys and serve piping hot.

Kidney Soup

Oxtail Sou

Cream of Carrot Soup

3 strips bacon, diced
2 tablespoons butter
1 pound carrots, peeled and finely chopped
1 stalk celery, finely chopped
1 cup diced turnip
1 small onion, finely chopped
3 tablespoons flour
6 cups chicken stock
1 cup milk
$\frac{1}{2}$ cup light cream
2 tablespoons finely chopped parsley

Fry the bacon until all the fat has rendered. Remove the bacon and leave to one side. Add the butter to 1 tablespoon of the bacon fat and sauté the vegetables for 5 minutes until softened. Stir in the flour. Stir in the chicken stock and simmer for 20 minutes. Rub through a strainer or purée in an electric blender. Return to the saucepan and heat until hot. Add the cream and garnish with bacon and parsley.

Mulligatawny Soup

2 pounds stewing lamb
8 cups water
4 beef bouillon cubes
$\frac{1}{2}$ cup pearl barley
1 onion, finely chopped
2 leeks, thinly sliced
1 carrot, finely chopped
1 stalk celery, thinly sliced
1 small turnip, peeled and diced
1 teaspoon salt
freshly ground black pepper
2 tablespoons finely chopped parsley

Heat the butter and sauté the vegetables, except the tomatoes, and apple for 5 minutes until softened. Stir in the curry powder and flour. Stir in the beef stock. Add the tomatoes and tomato paste. Add the cloves, sugar, salt and pepper. Simmer for 20 minutes. Add the milk, leftover meat or chicken and rice. Simmer for 5 minutes and serve piping hot.

Hare Soup

2 tablespoons butter
1 onion, finely chopped
1 carrot, finely chopped
2 stalks celery, finely chopped
1 green pepper, seeded and chopped
1 small green apple, peeled, cored and thinly sliced
1–2 tablespoons curry powder
2 tablespoons flour
6 cups beef stock
2 medium sized tomatoes, peeled, seeded and chopped
2 teaspoons tomato paste
2 cloves
1 teaspoon sugar
1 teaspoon salt
freshly ground black pepper
1 cup milk
1 cup leftover diced meat or chicken
$\frac{1}{2}$ cup cooked rice

The tough parts of a hare or rabbit can be used to make an excellent soup base. Place the legs, head and chopped carcass in a large saucepan. Add the onion, celery, carrot, turnip, parsley, bay leaf, thyme, peppercorns, salt and ham or bacon. Add the stock. Cover and simmer for 4 hours. Strain the stock. Heat the butter. Stir in the flour and add the stock gradually. Add the port, redcurrant jelly, lemon juice and leftover hare or rabbit. Heat until hot.

Scotch Broth

¼ pound bacon
2 tablespoons butter
2 small onions, finely chopped
¾ pound calf's liver
¼ cup flour
2 tablespoons butter
6 cups chicken broth
1 teaspoon salt
freshly ground black pepper
2 teaspoons lemon juice
teaspoons Worcestershire sauce
2 tablespoons finely chopped
parsley

Cut the lamb into 1″ cubes and place in a large saucepan. Add the water and bouillon cubes. Cover and simmer for 45 minutes. Add the barley and vegetables. Cover and simmer for 1 hour. Chill the soup overnight and skim off the fat that will rise to the surface. Heat until hot. Season with salt and pepper and garnish with parsley. The meat may be served in the soup or moistened with a little of the broth and eaten separately.

Liver and Bacon Soup

legs, head and carcass of a hare
or rabbit
1 onion, sliced
1 stalk celery, chopped
1 carrot, chopped
1 small turnip, chopped
3 sprigs parsley
1 bay leaf
1 teaspoon thyme
10 peppercorns
1 teaspoon salt
2 ounces ham or bacon, diced
10 cups beef stock
3 tablespoons butter
3 tablespoons four
½ cup port wine
1 tablespoon redcurrant jelly
2 teaspoons lemon juice
leftover cooked hare or rabbit

Fry the bacon until all the fat has rendered. Remove the bacon and leave to one side. Sauté the onions in the hot baconfat. Wash the liver. Pat dry on paper towels. Cut into bite sized pieces and dredge in flour. Add the butter to the pan with the onions and heat until hot. Sauté the liver in the hot fat. Add the chicken broth, salt, pepper, lemon juice and Worcestershire sauce. Simmer for 5 minutes and garnish with bacon and parsley.

Belgium

Anyone fortunate enough to be invited to dine in a Belgian home is in for a treat, especially as regards the soup, for the Belgians are the soup connoisseurs of northern Europe. Situated between Holland and France, Belgium in its cuisine combines the sensible simplicity of the Dutch with the artistry of the French. Belgian cooking tends to be well balanced, nutritious, and excellent, and Belgian cooks take justifiable pride in their regional specialties. They are renowned for their vast variety of endive dishes, and their sausages and hams are as fine as any, bar none. The food and delicacy shops that are to be found in every street of every Belgian town are a feast for the eye as well as the palate, and bustling market squares teem with mussels and oysters. A glass of wine or cold beer is the fitting accompaniment to every satisfying meal, and to top it all off, coffee and exquisite chocolates are always available.

Ghentian Waterzooi Soup

Ghentian Waterzooi Soup

2½ pound chicken
1 onion, sliced
2 carrots, sliced
1 leek sliced, or
1 additional onion
2 stalks celery, sliced
3 sprigs parsley
¼ teaspoon nutmeg
1 clove
1 teaspoon thyme
1 bay leaf
4 cups water
2 chicken bouillon cubes
1 tablespoon lemon juice
2 cups dry white wine
3 egg yolks
½ cup light cream
1 teaspoon salt
freshly ground black pepper

Put the chicken, vegetables, parsley, nutmeg, clove, thyme and bay leaf into a large kettle. Add the water, bouillon cubes and lemon juice and bring to the boil. Add the wine and simmer for 1 hour until the chicken is tender. Strip the meat from the bones and cut into small pieces. Strain the stock. Discard the parsley and bay leaf and reserve the vegetables. Stir the egg yolks with the cream and add to the warm stock. Do not reboil or the egg and cream mixture will curdle. Heat the soup to simmering point only. Put the chicken and cooked vegetables into warm soup plates and pour the hot broth over them. Serve with French bread.

Brussels Sprout Soup

2 tablespoons butter
1½ pounds Brussels sprouts, washed and drained
2 tablespoons flour
6 cups water
2 chicken bouillon cubes
1 teaspoon salt
freshly ground black pepper
¼ teaspoon ground nutmeg
2 egg yolks
1 cup light cream
2 cups croutons

Heat the butter and sauté the sprouts for 5 minutes. Stir in the flour, water and bouillon cubes. Season with salt and pepper. Add the nutmeg and simmer in a covered saucepan for 50 minutes. Rub the soup through a strainer or purée in an electric blender. Beat the egg yolks with the cream and add to the hot soup, stirring continuously. Just before serving, garnish with croutons.

Green Soup

3 tablespoons butter
2 leeks or onions, chopped
1 stalk celery, sliced
¼ pound sorrel or ½ pound
spinach, chopped
1 tablespoon fresh chervil or
1 teaspoon dried chervil
2 quarts water
4 bouillon cubes
2½ pounds potatoes, peeled
and diced
1 teaspoon salt
freshly ground black pepper

Heat the butter in a large saucepan. Add the vegetables and herbs. Cover and cook in the butter for 15 minutes. (Reserve a little of the sorrel and chervil for garnishing). Add the water and bouillon cubes, bring to the boil and add the potatoes. Simmer for 45 minutes. Rub the soup through a strainer or purée in an electric blender. Return to the saucepan and heat until hot. Season to taste and garnish with the reserved sorrel and chervil.

Green Soup

Ostend Lentil and Mussel Soup

½ pound lentils
6 cups water
1 bay leaf
1 stalk celery, thinly cliced
1 teaspoon salt
2 tablespoons butter
2 quarts fresh mussels, scrubbed
3 sprigs parsley
2 leeks or onions, thinly sliced
1 teaspoon salt
freshly ground black pepper
2 tablespoons parsley, finely chopped

This tasty, colorful, nourishing soup can be served as a main course.

Wash the lentils and soak them for 2 hours in the water. Add the bay leaf, celery and salt and bring to the boil. Simmer for 1 hour until the lentils are soft. Rub the soup through a strainer or purée in an electric blender.

Cut the butter into pieces and swirl into the soup. Scrub the mussels well and discard any that are open. Put the mussels into a large saucepan together with the parsley and leeks and add a little salt and pepper. Cover the pan and cook gently for 10 minutes, shaking the pan from time to time so as to distribute the liquid of the mussels evenly throughout the pan. When the mussels have opened, strain the liquid into the soup through several layers of cheesecloth. Remove the mussels from the shells. Add the mussels to the soup. Season to taste. Garnish with chopped parsley and serve with French bread and a salad.

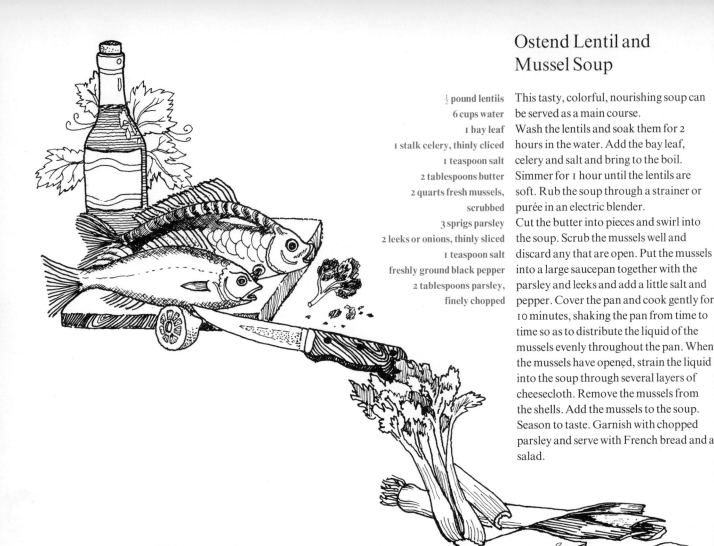

Waterzooi

½ pound fish bones and trimmings
4 cups water
2 cups dry white wine
strip of lemon peel
4 sprigs parsley
2 pounds fresh water fish fillets
½ teaspoon salt
2 tablespoons finely chopped parsley
2 tablespoons butter
4 slices bread, crusts removed

A traditional Belgian soup, it typifies Belgian cuisine. It is a combination of refinement of flavor and satisfying substance. Though it is traditionally made with fresh water fish, in Ghent chicken is used instead.

Put the fish bones, water, wine, lemon peel and parsley into a large kettle and bring to the boil. Cover and simmer for 30 minutes. Strain the stock. Add the fish fillets and salt and simmer for another 10 minutes until the fish is tender. Heat the butter and fry the bread until it is crisp and lightly browned. Put one slice into each bowl and fill the bowls with hot soup. Traditionally the fish is served separately, but it can be served together with the soup. Garnish with parsley.

Turnip Soup

½ pound turnips, peeled and thinly sliced
½ pound potatoes, peeled and diced
4 slices stale bread, crumbled
1 bay leaf
1 teaspoon salt
freshly ground black pepper
½ cup light cream
2 tablespoons finely chopped parsley

Bring the water to the boil and add the turnips, potatoes, bread, bay leaf, salt and pepper. Simmer for 1½ hours. Rub the soup through a strainer or purée in an electric blender. Return to the pan and simmer for another 10 minutes. Just before serving, stir in the cream and garnish with the chopped parsley.

Potato Soup

3 tablespoons butter
3 tablespoons flour
4 cups chicken stock
2½ pounds potatoes, diced
2 carrots, sliced
2 onions, chopped
⅛ teaspoon nutmeg
⅓ cup dry white wine
freshly ground black pepper
½ cup cooked peas
2 tablespoons finely chopped parsley
2 teaspoons chopped chives

Heat the butter in a saucepan. Stir in the flour and cook gently for 2 minutes. Do not brown. Add the stock gradually, stirring continuously. Add the potatoes and the remaining vegetables, nutmeg and wine. Cover and simmer for 30 minutes. Rub the soup through a strainer or purée in an electric blender. Return to the pan, simmer for another 15 minutes and season to taste. Add the peas and chopped herbs.

Flemish Buttermilk Soup

4 tablespoons flour
2 quarts buttermilk
¼ teaspoon salt
½ cup raisins
⅓ cup sugar
1 egg yolk
1 teaspoon vanilla extract
1 egg white, stiffly beaten

Buttermilk soup is served as a luncheon dish or as a dessert, (thinly sliced apples or soaked prunes may be substituted for the raisins).
Whisk the flour into the buttermilk, add the salt and raisins and bring the mixture slowly to the boil. Lower the heat and simmer gently for 10 minutes, stirring continuously. Beat the sugar with the egg yolk. Add the vanilla extract. Fold in the stiffly beaten egg white and gradually stir this mixture into the hot soup.

Onion Soup

4 tablespoons butter
4 medium sized onions, sliced
1 teaspoon salt
1 teaspoon sugar
2 cups beer
2 cups beef stock
2 teaspoons cornstarch
½ cup light cream

Heat the butter and sauté the onions gently for 10 minutes. Add the salt, sugar, beer and stock. Bring to the boil and simmer gently for 40 minutes. Stir in the cornstarch dissolved in the cream, and stir well. Simmer for 5 minutes until the soup has thickened slightly.

Flemish Vegetable Hodgepodge

1 pound cabbage, shredded
2 parsnips, peeled and diced
3 carrots, thinly sliced
2 stalks celery, thinly sliced
2 onions, chopped
2 bay leaves
6 peppercorns
1 pound pig's trotters
½ pound pork belly
2 pounds beef bones with scraps of beef
3 quarts water
2 pounds potatoes, peeled and sliced
1 teaspoon salt

This is a variation on a traditional Dutch recipe of mixed mashed vegetables and potatoes. Vegetable hodgepodge is usually served as a main course, but it can be strained, the broth mixed with puréed peas and then served as a first course. In that case, the meat and vegetables are not mashed but served as a main course, somewhat like the French pot au feu. Add the vegetables, bay leaves, peppercorns, meat, bones and meat scraps to the water. Cover and simmer for 2 hours. Add the potatoes and simmer for another 30 minutes. Season with salt, cut up the meat, mash the potatoes and vegetables (if necessary add some broth to make a thick soup). Season to taste and serve the soup and meat separately with toast and mustard.

Holland

Cloudy skies and wet wintry days are only too frequent in Holland, but it is always good to know that bowl of delicious hot soup awaits the returning traveller. The Dutch are great soup eaters and enjoy it all year round. In the winter months, nourishing bean and pea soups are served almost daily. In the spring there are soups brimming with every conceivable vegetable. Herbs are not used as extensively in Holland as in some other countries. This is not because of over-caution, but because the aim is to achieve the pure taste of the freshly cooked high quality vegetables. The last few years have seen a growth in the sale of packaged soups, but they are used only has a base. Every Dutch housewife has her own secret for brightening up dried or canned soups.

Soup is not only eaten in the comfort of the home, every café and restaurant has a 'soup of the day', so that a nourishing bowl of asparagus, mushroom, oxtail, chicken or tomato soup can be enjoyed at any time of the day.

Mussel Soup

2 quarts fresh mussels
5 cups water
2 tablespoons butter
1 carrot, thinly sliced
1 large onion, finely chopped
1 leek, thinly sliced
2 stalks celery, thinly sliced
3 chicken bouillon cubes
1 teaspoon salt
freshly ground black pepper
2 tablespoons finely chopped parsley

This is a mussel soup from the southernmost part of Holland.
Wash the mussels carefully under cold running water. Scrub the shells until they are clean. Discard any mussels that have opened. Place the mussels in a large saucepan. Add 1 cup of water. Cover the pan and steam the mussels until all the shells have opened. Strain the liquid from the pan through a colander lined with several thicknesses of cheesecloth. Reserve the cooking liquid. Remove a half shell from each mussel. Heat the butter and fry the vegetables gently until soft but not brown. Add the reserved cooking liquid and the remaining water. Stir in the bouillon cubes. Season with salt and pepper. Bring to boiling point and add the mussels. Allow the mussels to heat through and garnish the soup with parsley.

Cheese Soup

4 cups chicken stock
2 eggs
½ cup light cream
½ cup grated Gruyère or Swiss cheese
2 tablespoons finely chopped parsley

A simple yet delicious soup. Beat the eggs with the cream, cheese, and parsley. Heat the stock, add the beaten egg mixture, stirring constantly. Serve piping hot with breadsticks.

St. Hubert's Soup

St. Hubert's Soup
Game Soup

1 carcass, the feet and neck (with leftover meat) of a cooked wild duck, pheasant, goose or rabbit
1 pound lentils (soaked for 2 hours in sufficient water to cover them)
1 onion, chopped
1 teaspoon dried thyme
1 bay leaf
1 teaspoon salt
freshly ground black pepper
6 cups water
½ cup whipping cream

St. Hubert is the patron saint of hunters, so in Europe, his name is often given to game soup. This soup is very popular in Holland during the game season. Remove the cooked meat from the bones and keep a few of the well-shaped pieces to use as a garnish. Put the remaining scraps of meat and bones in a large saucepan with the lentils, onion, thyme and bay leaf. Season with salt and pepper. Add the water. Cover and simmer for about 1 hour, or until the lentils are soft and tender. Strain the soup and discard the bones and bay leaf. Rub the lentils, onion and meat through a strainer or purée in an electric blender. Add the strained stock gradually to the lentil purée. Reheat the soup and stir in the cream and remaining pieces of meat just before serving.

Right: Mussel Soup

44

Potato Soup

1½ pounds potatoes, peeled and cubed
2 leeks, thinly sliced
2 carrots, chopped
1 teaspoon salt
freshly ground black pepper
½ teaspoon dried marjoram
4 cups simmering chicken stock
1 cup milk
1 tablespoon butter
½ cup light cream
2 tablespoons finely chopped parsley
1 teaspoon dried chervil

Boil the potatoes, chopped vegetables and seasonings in the chicken stock for 30 minutes until tender. Rub through a strainer or purée in an electric blender. Add the warm stock and milk to the vegetable purée, stirring continuously. Return to the heat and simmer for 10 minutes. Stir in the butter and add the cream, chopped parsley and chervil just before serving.

Bean and Bacon Soup

¾ pound bacon or ham, diced
2 quarts water
1 pound green beans, sliced
6 medium sized potatoes, peeled, diced and boiled
6 sprigs parsley
1 beef bouillon cube

This specialty from the Brabant region is usually served as a main course. Fry the bacon or ham until crisp, pour off the drippings and add the crisped bacon or ham to the water. Add the beans, potatoes, parsley and bouillon cube. Simmer for 12 minutes, until the beans are tender and the broth has thickened slightly. Discard the parsley sprigs and serve hot.

Shrimp Soup

6 cups fish stock
$\frac{1}{4}$ cup rice flour, or
2 tablespoons cornstarch
$\frac{1}{2}$ cup light cream
$\frac{1}{2}$ teaspoon paprika
$\frac{1}{2}$ pound shrimp, cleaned
and cooked
2 tablespoons butter
1 teaspoon lemon juice
1 teaspoon salt
freshly ground black pepper
2 tablespoons finely chopped
parsley

Bring the stock to the boil. Blend the rice flour or cornstarch with the cream and paprika and add to the stock, stirring continuously. Simmer the soup for 15 minutes. Dice all but a handful of the shrimps and stir them into the soup together with the butter. Add the lemon juice. Season with salt and pepper and garnish with the remaining whole shrimps and chopped parsley.

Thick Pea Soup

1 pound split peas
2 quarts water
3 cloves
1 whole onion, peeled
2 pigs trotters, or $\frac{1}{2}$ pound
slice of ham
1$\frac{1}{2}$ teaspoons salt
freshly ground black pepper
1 bay leaf
1 teaspoon thyme
4 leeks, thinly sliced
2 stalks celery, chopped
3 medium-sized potatoes,
peeled
and chopped
$\frac{3}{4}$ pound Polish sausage
$\frac{1}{2}$ pound bacon, preferably
unsmoked
8 slices rye or brown bread
mustard
2 tablespoons chopped parsley

This chunky soup is usually served as a main course. Any leftover soup can be diluted with chicken broth the next day and eaten as a first course. As a matter of fact, Dutch pea soup often tastes even better the next day.
Wash the peas and let them soak overnight in 2 quarts of cold water. (This step may be eliminated with some dried peas. Follow the directions on the package.) Bring the peas to the boil in the water in which they have soaked. Stick the cloves into the whole peeled onion and add to the peas together with the pig's trotters or ham, salt, pepper, bay leaf and thyme. Cover the pan and simmer the soup for about 2 hours, until the peas are soft and tender. Discard the onion with cloves and bay leaf. Rub the soup through a strainer or purée in an electric blender. Add the remaining prepared vegetables, potatoes, sausage and bacon. Return the soup to boiling point and simmer for another 45 minutes stirring occasionally. If the soup seems too thick, add a little extra water.
Cut the sausage into $\frac{1}{4}''$ thick slices, remove the meat from the pig's trotters and return it to the soup. Spread the bread with mustard, cut the bacon into small pieces and arrange on top of the bread. Sprinkle the soup with chopped parsley and serve the bread and soup as a main course.

Asparagus Soup

1 bunch (approximately 1
pound)
asparagus, cut into 1″ pieces
4 cups water
2 tablespoons butter
2 tablespoons flour
1 egg yolk
$\frac{1}{2}$ cup light cream
$\frac{1}{4}$ teaspoon ground nutmeg
1 teaspoon salt
freshly ground black pepper

Cook the asparagus in the water until tender for 10–12 minutes. Strain and reserve the liquid. Melt the butter in a saucepan, stir in flour, cook gently for 2 minutes and continue to stir until smooth. Do not allow the flour mixture to brown. Gradually add the reserved liquid, stirring continuously. Bring to the boil, turn down the heat, and cook gently for about 15 minutes. Meanwhile, beat the egg yolk together with the cream, add the nutmeg. Stir a few spoonfuls of the hot soup into the beaten egg, and gradually stir this mixture into the simmering soup. Season with salt and pepper. Be careful not to let the soup boil or it will curdle. Add the cooked asparagus and garnish with fried croutons.

46

Brown Bean Soup

1 pound dried brown beans
2 quarts water
1 bay leaf
2 cloves
2 teaspoons chili powder
2 medium sized potatoes, peeled
1 onion, finely chopped
2 stalks celery, thinly sliced
4 tablespoons butter
1 teaspoon Worcestershire sauce
2 tablespoons finely chopped parsley

Brown bean soup, like thick pea soup, can also be served as a main course. Wash the beans and soak them in the cold water overnight. Add the bay leaf, cloves and chili to the water. Add the beans and simmer for 1 hour or until the beans are tender. Add the potatoes and simmer for another 30 minutes. Sauté the onion and celery in the butter. Rub the soup through a strainer or purée in an electric blender. Add the chopped onion and celery to the soup, return to the saucepan, and cook gently for 20 minutes, stirring occasionally. Season with salt, pepper and Worcestershire sauce. Sprinkle with chopped parsley and serve with bread or toast.

Leek and Potato Soup

6 cups chicken stock
2 leeks, thinly sliced
¼ cup uncooked rice
2 onions, finely chopped
3 large potatoes, diced
1 teaspoon salt
freshly ground black pepper

This is a regional soup from the southern part of Brabant. Leftover meat or sausage is often added and the dish is served as a main course.
Bring the stock to the boil, add the leeks, rice, onions and potatoes and cook for 30 minutes. Rub the soup through a strainer or purée in an electric blender. Season with salt and pepper and serve with rye or brown bread and cheese.

Hare Soup

the feet, head, carcass and giblets
of a hare or rabbit
3 quarts water
2 onions, chopped
1 carrot
4 sprigs parsley
¼ teaspoon mace
1 bay leaf
2 cloves
4 juniper berries
1 teaspoon thyme
1 teaspoon salt
4 tablespoons butter
4 tablespoons flour
freshly ground black pepper
¼ teaspoon ground cloves
¼ teaspoon nutmeg
2 tablespoons Madeira or
¼ cup red wine
2 teaspoons Worcestershire sauce
½ cup light cream
leftover meat from a roast hare or
rabbit, diced
leftover gravy or sauce

A spicy soup popular in the south of Holland. Make a rich game stock from the feet, head, carcass and giblets of the hare. Add the water, 1 of the onions, carrot, parsley, mace, bay leaf, cloves, juniper berries, thyme and salt and simmer in a partially covered pot for 4 hours. Strain. Sauté the remaining chopped onion in the butter for 2 minutes. Stir in the flour, pepper, ground cloves and nutmeg. Stir to form a smooth paste and stir in the stock. Cook gently for 10 minutes. Strain once more and add the Madeira or wine, Worcestershire sauce and cream. Add any leftover meat and gravy or sauce.

Vegetable Soup with Meatballs

3 tablespoon butter
4 stalks celery, sliced
12 Brussels sprouts
1 leek or onion, chopped
1 carrot, diced
6 cups beef stock
½ teaspoon thyme
2 ounces thin noodles
¼ pound beef or veal, ground
½ teaspoon salt
freshly ground black pepper
1 slice bread, soaked in
¼ cup milk
2 teaspoons arrowroot or cornstarch, dissolved in 2 tablespoons cold water
1½ tablespoons parsley or chervil, finely chopped

Heat the butter in a large saucepan. Add the vegetables and toss to coat well. Cook gently for 10 minutes. Bring the stock to the boil, pour over the braised vegetables, add the thyme and the noodles. Simmer for 30 minutes.
Season the beef or veal with salt and pepper. Combine with the soaked bread and form into small meatballs. Add these to the soup during the last 10 minutes of cooking. To thicken the soup (optional), dissolve the arrowroot or cornstarch in the water and stir into the broth. Season to taste and serve sprinkled with chopped parsley or chervil.

Barley Soup

Mushroom Soup

Bean and Tomato Soup

½ pound dried white beans
6 cups water
3 tablespoons butter
1 leek, thinly sliced
1 teaspoon salt
1 bay leaf
⅛ teaspoon mace
2 ounces bacon, diced
1 tablespoon tomato paste
¼ cup light cream or milk
1 teaspoon salt
freshly ground black pepper
2 tablespoons finely chopped parsley

Wash and soak the beans overnight in the water. Heat 1 tablespoon of the butter and cook the leek gently for 5 minutes. Put the beans and water into a large saucepan, add the leek, salt, bay leaf and mace and bring to the boil. Cover and simmer for 1½ hours. Add the bacon and simmer for another 15 minutes. Cut the remaining 2 tablespoons of butter into small pieces and swirl into the soup. Stir in the tomato paste and cream or milk and serve seasoned to taste. Garnish with parsley.

Bean and Tomato Soup

Barley Soup

¼ cup barley
4 cups water
1 teaspoon salt
¾ pound Polish sausage
½ cup raisins
1 teaspoon dried mint or
1 tablespoon fresh mint, chopped
1 cup buttermilk
2 tablespoons finely chopped parsley
1 teaspoon chervil

This is a regional specialty of the Gelderland and Overijssel regions of eastern Holland. It is often served as a main course and sometimes even as a dessert, with molasses.
Soak the barley overnight in the water, add the salt, and bring to the boil. Cover and simmer for 1 hour. Add the sausage and simmer for another 30 minutes. Remove and slice the sausage. Stir in the raisins and mint and simmer the soup for another 15 minutes. Return the sausage to the soup, stir in the buttermilk and garnish with chopped parsley and chervil.

Mushroom Soup

2 tablespoons butter
5 ounces mushrooms, sliced
2 tablespoons shallots or scallions
2 tablespoons flour
4 cups chicken stock, hot
juice of 1 lemon or
¼ cup white wine
½ teaspoon salt
freshly ground black pepper
¼ cup heavy cream

Heat the butter in a saucepan, sauté the mushrooms and shallots until soft, but do not brown. Stir in the flour and add the hot stock gradually, stirring continuously. Cover and simmer for 10 minutes. Add the lemon juice or wine. Season with salt and pepper and stir in the cream just before serving.

Chicken Soup with Meatballs

3 lb. chicken cut into serving pieces
2 quarts water
¼ teaspoon nutmeg
1 teaspoon chili powder
1 bay leaf
½ teaspoon basil
2 carrots, sliced
5 sprigs parsley
4 tablespoons butter
4 tablespoons flour
¼ cup uncooked rice
¼ pound veal or beef, ground
½ slice bread, soaked in
¼ cup milk
1 teaspoon salt
freshly ground black pepper
¼ cup light cream
2 tablespoons finely chopped parsley

Place the chicken in a large saucepan and add the water, nutmeg, chili powder, bay leaf, basil, carrots and parsley. Cover and cook gently for 2½ hours. Strain the broth. Strip the white meat from the bones and cut lengthwise into tiny pieces. Cool the stock and skim off the fat that will rise to the surface. Heat the butter, stir in the flour and cook gently for 2 minutes. Gradually add the strained, degreased stock and the rice and simmer for 15 minutes. Add the chicken pieces. Meanwhile mix the ground meat and bread, season with salt and pepper, and form into ½″ balls. Just before serving add the meatballs to the soup and simmer for 10 minutes. Stir in the cream and chopped parsley.

49

Cold Cherry Soup

1 pound cherries, pitted
2 cups red wine
2 cups water, or 1 cup dry white
wine and 1 cup water
½ cup sugar
grated rind 1 orange
1 tablespoon arrowroot or
cornstarch
2 tablespoons cold water
1 cup whipped cream or 6
meringues

Chilled fruit soup is a delicious treat on a hot summer day. It can be served either as an appetizer or for dessert. If you enjoy grapefruit or melon for a first course, try a German fruit soup for a change.

Place the cherries into a saucepan. Add the wine, water, sugar and orange rind. Cover and simmer gently for 10 minutes. Rub through a strainer or purée in an electric blender. Bring to the boil. Mix the arrowroot or cornstarch with the water and stir into the soup. Simmer for 2 minutes until the soup is thick and smooth. Chill for 4 hours and serve garnished either with a spoonful of cream or top with a meringue.

Germany

Throughout the years the German cuisine has had a reputation of being somewhat heavy, but recently there have been many changes. Today few German women have time to prepare the traditional national foods, though they do still follow their customary pattern of eating the main meal in the middle of the day. In the evening they have a light supper usually on the order of open-faced sandwiches and a salad. Hearty soups are served frequently as the main course at midday. Each region has its own specialty and every soup lover has a particular favorite. One of these, the choice of many fish and seafood fanciers, and one of Germany's most popular soups is the famous Hamburg eel soup. On an entirely different order, there are sweet fruit soups that are served either hot or cold either as a first course or for dessert.

Allgäuer Soup with Liver Dumplings

⅓ pound beef liver, ground
2 slices day-old white bread,
crusts removed
2 tablespoons grated hard
cheese
2 tablespoons finely chopped
parsley
2 tablespoons milk
1 tablespoon softened butter
1 teaspoon salt
freshly ground black pepper
2 eggs
⅓ cup breadcrumbs
5 cups beef stock

Mix all the ingredients lightly except the stock and form into a firm mixture, adding a few more breadcrumbs if necessary. Chill for 20 minutes. Using two teaspoons, shape the chilled mixture into small dumplings. Bring the stock to boiling point. Reduce the heat and poach the dumplings in the simmering stock for 10 minutes.

Westphalian Buttermilk Soup

4 cups buttermilk
¼ cup sugar
3 slices German pumpernickel
bread, made into breadcrumbs
¾ cup raisins soaked in hot
water for 2 minutes and drained
1 teaspoon powdered cinnamon

This buttermilk soup is a favorite dessert in Eastern Friesland and Westphalia. Heat the buttermilk to the boiling point. Add the sugar and stir until the sugar has dissolved. Add the breadcrumbs and raisins. Stir in the cinnamon and simmer gently for 5 minutes. Serve hot.

Salsify Soup

4 tablespoons butter
¼ pound smoked shoulder of pork, finely chopped
½ pound salsify, chopped
5 cups beef stock
4 large potatoes, peeled and grated
⅛ teaspoon nutmeg
½ teaspoon salt
freshly ground black pepper
⅓ cup sour cream
2 tablespoons finely chopped parsley

Heat the butter and sauté the pork and salsify for about 5 minutes. Add the stock, potatoes, nutmeg, salt and pepper. Simmer gently for 20 minutes. Stir in the sour cream. Garnish with parsley. Salsify is a popular vegetable in Germany but rather difficult to find in America. Substitute any other fresh vegetable in season.

Carnival Soup

½ cup olive oil
1½ pounds shoulder of pork, finely diced
7 medium sized onions sliced
2 tablespoons curry powder
2 cups chicken stock
2 tablespoons lemon juice
4 cups milk
¾ cup dried apricots, chopped
2 tablespoons raisins
2 small apples, peeled, cored and grated
2 tablespoons soy sauce
¼ cup red wine
½ teaspoon salt

After a night of mardi-gras revelry a cup of this soup drunk at dawn, makes a great pick-me-up.
Heat the oil and fry the pork quickly on all sides until lightly browned. Stir in the onions and curry powder and cook gently for 5 minutes. Add the chicken stock, lemon juice and milk and simmer for 1 hour. During the last 15 minutes, add the apricots and raisins. Add the grated apples and cook for the last 5 minutes. Season to taste with the soy sauce, wine and salt.

North German Lentil Soup

1 pound lentils
9 cups water
1 pound smoked pork, diced
1 clove garlic, chopped
1 bay leaf
½ cup bacon, diced
2 onions, chopped
1 pound pitted prunes, soaked in tea overnight and drained
4 medium sized potatoes, peeled and diced
1 teaspoon salt
freshly ground black pepper
½ teaspoon basil
3 tablespoons vinegar
2 teaspoons sugar
¼ cup red wine (optional)

The people of northern Germany are very fond of sweet and sour dishes. A favorite of the region combines brown beans, fresh pears, dried fruit and bacon. The prunes in this recipe may be omitted without seriously impairing the flavor of the soup.
Soak the lentils overnight in the water. Add the pork, garlic and bay leaf and cook over a low heat for 20 minutes. Fry the bacon. Remove and leave to one side and add the onions to the bacon fat. Fry the onions for 3 minutes. Add the soaked prunes to the soup and simmer for 15 minutes. Add the potatoes, bacon, onions, season with salt and pepper and add the basil, vinegar and sugar. Simmer gently for 30 minutes. Add the wine just before serving. Serve with freshly made toast.

Sausage Soup

4 onions, sliced
4 medium sized potatoes, peeled and diced
6 cups beef stock
¼ teaspoon nutmeg
2 tablespoons finely chopped parsley
¼ pound blood pudding or other German sausage
¼ pound liverwurst, diced
2 tablespoons finely chopped chives

This soup, served with dark bread and a cold glass of beer, makes a substantial main course.
Boil the onions and potatoes in the stock for 25 minutes. Stir in the nutmeg and parsley. Add the blood pudding or sausage and liverwurst during the last 5 minutes. Garnish with chives and serve hot.

Prussian Cabbage Soup

8 cups water
1 pound spare ribs
½ pound bacon, diced
1 bay leaf
freshly ground black pepper
2 chicken bouillon cubes
4 cups cabbage, shredded
4 medium sized potatoes, peeled and diced
1 tablespoon flour
½ cup sour cream
2 tablespoons vinegar
½ teaspoon sugar

This soup is sufficiently substantial to make a satisfying main course.

Put the water, meat, bacon, bay leaf, pepper and bouillon cubes into a large saucepan. Bring to boiling point, lower the heat and simmer for 45 minutes. Strain and reserve the meat. Chill the broth and remove the fat that will rise to the surface. Return the broth to the heat, add the cabbage and potatoes and simmer for 45 minutes. After 35 minutes add the meat from the spareribs and bacon. Stir the flour with the sour cream, vinegar and sugar and stir into the soup. Simmer for another 10 minutes and serve with sliced German bread.

Bavarian Beer Soup

4 cups light beer
peel of 1 lemon
1 cup raisins, soaked in hot water for 5 minutes and drained
2 egg yolks
¼ cup sugar
½ cup heavy cream, stiffly whipped
1 teaspoon salt
freshly ground black pepper
1 cup croutons

Bring the beer and lemon peel to the boil. Add the raisins and simmer for 5 minutes. Combine the egg yolks and sugar and fold into the stiffly beaten cream. Discard the lemon peel, and stir a few spoonfuls of the hot beer into the egg and cream mixture. Return to the hot beer. Season with salt and pepper and serve with croutons.

Hamburg Eel Soup

Hamburg Eel Soup

3 pounds fish bones and trimmings
1 piece bacon rind and
½ pound cooked bacon, diced
10 cups water
2 leeks or 1 large extra onion, chopped
2 onions, chopped
2 carrots, diced
½ celery root, diced or
2 stalks celery, sliced
¼ pound mixed dried fruits, e.g. pears, apples prunes, etc.
3 sprigs parsley
1 bay leaf
½ teaspoon thyme
½ teaspoon summer savory
½ teaspoon basil
¼ teaspoon tarragon
8 ounce package frozen green peas
¼ cup wine vinegar
2 pounds fresh or smoked eel, into 2″ segments cut
1 tablespoon sugar
1 tablespoon lemon juice
1 teaspoon salt
freshly ground black pepper
2 tablespoons freshly chopped parsley

Place the fish bones and trimmings with the bacon rind and diced bacon into a saucepan. Add the water. Cover and simmer for 1 ½ hours. Strain the broth and skim off the fat that will rise to the surface. Add the vegetables, dried fruit, parsley, bay leaf and herbs and simmer gently for 30 minutes until the vegetables have cooked through. After 20 minutes add the peas. During the last 5 minutes add the vinegar, eel, sugar and lemon juice. Season with salt and pepper and garnish with the chopped parsley.

Rose Hip Soup

Rose Hip Soup

1 pound rose hips, tops removed, cut in halves and seeds discarded
5 cups water
2 teaspoons arrowroot or cornstarch dissolved in
2 tablespoons cold water
½ cup red wine (optional)
1 tablespoon slivered almonds
½ teaspoon salt
¾ cup sugar

This sweet fruit soup can be served either hot or cold as a first course or for dessert. Simmer the rose hips gently in the water for about 1 hour or until tender. Combine the arrowroot or cornstarch with the water and stir into the soup. Bring to the boil and cook gently for 10 minutes. Season with salt, add the sugar and the wine if used. Garnish with slivered almonds.

Note: Arrowroot gives the soup a clearer brighter color and should be used in preference to cornstarch if it is available. It can often be found among the spices in the supermarket.

Scandinavia

Soup, both pungent and sweet are popular throughout the Scandinavian countries. Meals in Scandinavia are often family affairs, and so many of the recipes found in Swedish, Norwegian, Danish and Finnish cookbooks are for more than four servings, providing enough to feed parents, children, relatives and friends.

Fish soup, apple soup, fruit and beer and bread soups are among the most popular Scandinavian soups, but Sweden has one local specialty uniquely her own; the Svartsoppa (Black Soup), served in celebration of St. Martin's Day, November 11. Families, friends and neighbors gather round to eat this substantial combination of goose, pork, pork ribs, vegetables, dried fruit and wine. There is nothing like a bowl of Svartsoppa and some rye bread to keep a gathering of Swedes content for an evening.

Norwegian Cold Fish Soup

2 pounds assorted fish, i.e. cod, haddock, trout etc.
2 onions, peeled and cut into quarters
1 clove garlic
1 cup sour cream
$\frac{1}{2}$ teaspoon salt
freshly ground black pepper
1 tablespoon chopped chives
$\frac{1}{2}$ teaspoon tarragon

The cooked fish from this delicious soup can be served separately or made into fish cakes for another meal.

Put the fish into a large saucepan together with the onions and garlic. Add sufficient cold water to cover. Bring to the boil. Reduce the heat and simmer until the fish flakes easily and is white and opaque. Strain the broth and chill it for 4 hours. Stir in the sour cream and season with the salt and pepper. Garnish with chives and tarragon.

Pea Soup

1 pound dried yellow or green split peas
10 cups water
$\frac{3}{4}$ pound lean salt pork
1 stalk celery, chopped
3 carrots, sliced
4 leeks or 2 additional onions, sliced
4 medium sized potatoes, peeled and sliced
2 small onions
6 sprigs fresh thyme or
1 teaspoon dried thyme
1 pound Polish sausage

In Denmark this soup is usually made with green peas but in Finland, Norway and Sweden, yellow peas are preferred. For no apparent reason the soup is usually eaten on Thursdays. It is a thick creamy soup and delicious served with rye bread that has been spread with mustard. Scandinavians tend to prefer homemade mustard containing vinegar or lemon juice and a dash of dried horseradish to the commercial brands.

To prepare the soup, soak the peas overnight in the water. Bring to the boil, add the salt pork, and simmer for 2 hours until the peas are soft and tender. Strain the soup and rub the peas through a strainer or purée in an electric blender. Cook the remaining vegetables, thyme and sausage in the stock for 20 minutes until tender. Strain once again and chop the vegetables into smaller pieces. Skim off any fat that has risen to the surface of the stock. Stir in the pea purée and chopped vegetables. Slice the sausage and serve separately with the bread and mustard.

Beer Soup

2 cups brown breadcrumbs
2 cups rye breadcrumbs
2 tablespoons sugar
1 tablespoon vanilla extract
4 cups water
4 cups dark beer
grated rind 1 lemon
1 tablespoon lemon juice
2 teaspoons powdered sugar
3 teaspoons cinnamon
1 teaspoon salt
1 egg yolk
$\frac{1}{2}$ cup heavy cream, whipped

Soak the breadcrumbs, sugar and vanilla for 1 hour in the water. Bring the mixture to the boil and simmer, stirring occasionally until the broth thickens. Add half of the beer, the grated lemon rind and juice, powdered sugar, cinnamon and salt. Simmer gently for 5 minutes. Stir the egg yolk into the remaining beer and add to the hot soup, stirring constantly. Heat until hot. Garnish with a heaping spoonful of whipped cream and serve hot.

Black Soup
Svartsoppa

the giblets of 5 freshly killed
geese
6 pounds goose bones and pork
ribs
5 cups carrots, chopped
5 cups leeks or onions, sliced
5 cups celery, diced
10 peppercorns
10 cups water
4 cups goose or pig blood
4 tablespoons vinegar
1 cup flour
4 cups apples, peeled, cored and
quartered
2 tablespoons sugar
1 cup dried prunes
1 teaspoon cinnamon
½ teaspoon ground cloves
1½ teaspoon ground ginger
1 tablespoon salt
2 tablespoons sugar
2 cups red wine
¼ cup Cognac

St. Martin's Day, celebrated on November 11th, is the most beloved of all Swedish feast days. It is the day for eating the Svartsoppa, made with the blood of freshly killed geese and pigs. Green or yellow dried split peas may be substituted for the vegetables in the above recipe. This dish is never made for just the family. Friends and neighbors are asked to share the treat.

Simmer the giblets, bones, ribs, vegetables and peppercorns in the water for 2 hours. Strain the soup and mix the blood with the vinegar and flour. Heat this mixture gently over low heat, stirring constantly until it begins to thicken. Do not allow it to boil or the blood will coagulate. Poach the apples with the sugar in a little water for 25 minutes until soft. Simmer the prunes for 25 minutes. Strain both fruits, and add all the liquid to the stock. Bring to the boil with the cinnamon, cloves and ginger. While stirring with a wire whisk, gradually blend in the blood mixture. This process should take 15–20 minutes. Add the salt, sugar, wine and Cognac. Cut the giblets into small pieces and stir them into the soup with the prunes and apples. Serve the soup with rye bread.

This soup is of course impossible to make unless you have freshly killed geese. However, it is so important a national soup that the recipe has been included in this collection for the interest of the reader.

Swedish Bread Soup

2 tablespoons butter
1 tablespoon flour
6 cups chicken stock
4 slices dark bread, made into
crumbs
1 sprig mint
1 tablespoon sugar
½ cup light cream
2 tablespoons butter
1 (6 ounce) can cocktail
sausages

Heat the butter, stir in the flour and add the stock gradually. Add the bread and mint and simmer gently for 15 minutes. Strain the broth. Stir in the sugar and add the cream, remaining butter and sausages. Heat the soup but do not allow it to boil.

Danish Apple Soup

2 pounds cooking apples,
unpeeled
and cut into quarters
4 cups chicken stock
Grated rind and juice of 1
lemon
1 cinnamon stick
1 teaspoon salt
½ cup Danish blue cheese,
crumbled
2 tablespoons cornstarch
½ cup cold water
½ cup dry white wine
4 zwieback rusks

Fruit soups are equally good served hot or cold. If served hot, sprinkle with freshly grated nutmeg; if served cold garnish with a spoonful of whipped cream. Since this recipe calls for blue cheese, this particular version is better served hot. Sugar and cinnamon may be substituted for the cheese. This soup is particularly good when accompanied by cucumber salad and Danish crispbread.

Combine the apples, chicken stock, grated lemon rind and juice, cinnamon stick, salt and cheese and bring to the boil. Simmer gently for 30 minutes, stirring occasionally until the apples are tender. Discard the cinnamon stick. Rub the soup through a strainer or purée in sn electric blender. Stir the cornstarch into the cold water and stir into the soup. Add the wine. Simmer gently for 10 minutes until thick and creamy. Crumble the zwieback, put a little into each serving bowl and add the hot soup.

Tomato Soup with Shimp

Tomato Soup with Shrimp

3 tablespoons butter
1 onion, finely chopped
3 ripe tomatoes, peeled, seeded and chopped
3 tablespoons flour
6 cups water
4 chicken bouillon cubes
8 ounce package frozen peas
½ pound shelled and deveined shrimp
1 teaspoon salt
freshly ground black pepper

Heat the butter and sauté the onion for 3 minutes. Add the tomatoes and cook for 10 minutes. Stir in the flour and add the water gradually. Add the bouillon cubes. Simmer gently for 30 minutes. Rub the soup through a strainer or purée in an electric blender. Add the peas and the shrimp. Season with salt and pepper and heat until hot.

Fruit Soup

1 cup mixed dried fruit with a maximum of 6 prunes
2 tablespoons butter
1 tablespoon curry powder
6 cups chicken stock
1 teaspoon lemon peel, grated
1 tablespoon cornstarch dissolved in
2 tablespoons cold water
½ cup sour cream
2 tablespoons fresh ginger root, minced

Fruit soups are so popular in Scandinavia that one food processing company has begun to market dehydrated rose hip soup. Because fresh fruit is scarce and expensive during the long winter months, dried fruit is a popular ingredient in many soups. Like other fruit soups, this one is eaten either hot or cold and either as a first course or instead of a more traditional dessert. For dessert, the soup is often served in tall glasses.

Soak the dried fruit overnight in hot tea. Strain the fruit. Heat the butter and add the curry powder. Add the chicken stock. Add the dried fruit and lemon peel and simmer for 30 minutes. Rub through a strainer or purée in an electric blender. Return the soup to a clean saucepan and bring to boiling point. Stir in the cornstarch dissolved in cold water and simmer for 2 minutes. Garnish the soup with a spoonful of sour cream and sprinkle with ginger root.

Finnish Fish Soup

3 medium sized potatoes
1 teaspoon salt
3 cups water
2 pounds fish fillets, cut into bite sized pieces
4 tablespoons butter
3 tablespoons flour
2 cups milk
1 chicken bouillon cube
1 teaspoon salt
freshly ground black pepper
1 tablespoon lemon juice
3 tablespoons finely chopped parsley or
2 tablespoons finely chopped chives or dillweed
1 tablespoon caviar or fish roe (optional)

Boil the potatoes for 10 minutes in the salted water. Add the fish and cook for another 10 minutes. Heat the butter, stir in the flour and cook for 2 minutes. Add the milk gradually and simmer gently for 10 minutes. Stir this white sauce into the soup and add the bouillon cube. Simmer for 3 minutes, season with salt and pepper and add the lemon juice. Garnish with parsley, chives or dill and caviar or fish roe.

Cabbage Soup

Mina's Lemon Soup

2 tablespoons butter
2 tablespoons flour
4 cups water
grated rind 2 small lemons
strained juice 2 small lemons
3 egg yolks
5 tablespoons sugar
2 egg whites stiffly beaten
½ teaspoon cinnamon

This soup can be eaten either hot or cold. In Denmark it is usually served as a dessert with wafer thin almond cakes or garnished with grated almonds. It also makes a delicious first course though the almonds should be eliminated if it is served at the beginning of a meal.
Heat the butter, stir in the flour and cook for 1 minute. Stir in the water gradually and add the grated lemon rind and juice. Beat the egg yolks with 3 tablespoons sugar and stir into the soup. Fold the remaining sugar into the beaten egg whites. Pour the soup into serving bowls. Spoon the egg whites into each bowl and sprinkle with cinnamon.

Cabbage Soup

6 thick slices bacon, diced
5 cups cabbage, shredded
4 carrots, sliced
2 leeks or 1 large onion, sliced
4 potatoes, diced
5 cups water
3 chicken bouillon cubes
½ teaspoon salt
freshly ground black pepper
2 tablespoons finely chopped parsley

Fry the bacon until all the fat has rendered. Add the cabbage, carrots and leeks or onion, and cook gently in a covered saucepan for 10 minutes. Add the potatoes, boiling water and bouillon cubes. Simmer for 30 minutes. Season with salt and pepper and garnish with parsley.

Central Europe

Traditionally the wealthiest countries of the world have a richer and more varied cuisine than those that are economically deprived. The cooking of Vienna has become an amalgam of the national dishes from the far-flung Hapsburg empire. Each dish has been changed slightly to suit the Austrian taste, but it is easy to see the association with the original prototype.

An Austrian meal usually starts with a soup that contains noodles, the soup is followed by a meat course accompanied by potatoes and a seasonal vegetable. The meal is completed with a cooked pudding, fresh fruit or cake.

Before the last war, Hungary was famous for the excellence of its cuisine but today, with more and more women working outside of the home, time consuming preparations have given way to quicker and less elaborate meals. Hungarian restaurants still serve authentic Hungarian dishes and the correct way to begin a traditional Hungarian meal is with a goulash soup.

The Polish cuisine is similar to that of Russia but bears more traces of the western influence. Polish menus contain Jewish, Austrian, Slavic and German dishes, but like their Russian neighbors, Poles are likely to start their meals with borsht, the traditional red beet soup.

Hungarian Goulash Soup

1 green pepper, finely chopped
1 onion, finely chopped
1 medium sized, tomato, peeled, seeded and chopped
2 tablespoons oil
3 onions, finely chopped
2 tablespoons oil
1 tablespoon paprika
$\frac{1}{8}$ teaspoon cayenne pepper
$\frac{1}{2}$ pound lean ground beef
1 clove garlic, finely chopped
$\frac{1}{2}$ teaspoon caraway seeds
6 cups water
4 beef bouillon cubes
$\frac{1}{2}$ teaspoon salt
4 medium sized potatoes, peeled and diced

Sauté the green pepper, 1 onion, and tomato in hot oil for 3 minutes and reserve. (In Hungary, suet is used instead of oil and the mixture is called *lesco*). Sauté the 3 remaining onions in hot oil for 5 minutes. Add the paprika, cayenne pepper, beef, garlic, and caraway seeds. Add the water, bouillon cubes and salt. Cover and simmer for $1\frac{1}{2}$ hours. During the last 30 minutes of cooking add the potatoes. Add the reserved pepper, onion and tomato mixture and heat until hot.

Bouillon with Liver Dumplings

$\frac{1}{4}$ pound chicken, calf's or lamb's liver, ground
$\frac{1}{2}$ onion, finely chopped
1 egg yolk
$\frac{1}{4}$ teaspoon salt
freshly ground black pepper
$\frac{1}{4}$ teaspoon thyme
$\frac{1}{8}$ teaspoon nutmeg
2 tablespoons finely chopped parsley
$1\frac{1}{2}$ slices bread, trimmed
2 tablespoons cold water
2 tablespoons flour
4 cups chicken stock

Combine the liver and onion. Stir in the egg yolk, salt, pepper, thyme, nutmeg and parsley. Soak the bread in the water. Squeeze dry and add to the liver mixture with sufficient flour to form a smooth, firm mixture. Bring the stock to the boiling point. Reduce the heat and maintain at simmering point. Shape the liver mixture into small balls and add to the soup. Simmer for 10 minutes. When the liver dumplings are cooked through they will rise to the surface of the stock.

Bouillon

4 cups homemade beef stock
4 raw or lightly poached eggs

Break an egg into each individual soup bowl and cover with hot stock. Few soups could be simpler or more nourishing.

Golem's Soup with Dumplings

3 tablespoons flour
1 teaspoon salt
3 tablespoons butter
3 egg yolks
1 tablespoon caraway seeds
4 cups beef or chicken stock
grated hard cheese (optional)

This Czech soup is named for the robot built by a medieval Prague rabbi. Legend has it that as time went on, the good rabbi lost control over his invention who roamed the streets of the city wreaking havoc wherever he went. Ultimately the creator caught up with the robot and destroyed him. Why this popular soup should be named after so fearful a creature is a mystery we shall not attempt to unravel.

Sift the flour with the salt into a large bowl. Beat the butter until soft and blend with the egg yolks. Stir this mixture into the flour and add the caraway seeds. Use a wooden spoon to beat the mixture until smooth. Form the mixture into dumplings. Traditionally they are rather large, but they can be any size you prefer. Bring the stock to boiling point. Reduce the heat and add the dumplings. Cook for 5–8 minutes until they rise to the surface of the broth. Just before serving the soup may be sprinkled with a little grated cheese.

Austrian Sauerkraut Soup

1 pound sauerkraut
6 cups beef stock
3 slices bacon, diced
1 onion, sliced
3 teaspoons tomato paste
1 teaspoon paprika
½ teaspoon caraway seeds
1 medium sized potato, peeled and diced
12 cocktail sausages

This popular soup has been a local favorite for centuries and enjoyed by rich and poor alike.

Simmer the sauerkraut in 2 cups of the stock for 30 minutes until tender. Fry the bacon. Remove and leave to one side. Fry the onion in the bacon fat until crisp. Add the tomato paste, paprika, caraway seeds and remaining stock. Simmer gently for 10 minutes. Pour this mixture over the sauerkraut. Add the potato and cook for another 20 minutes. Slice the sausages lengthwise and add to the soup. Heat until hot.

Hungarian Calf's Brain Soup

1 calf's brain
1 tablespoon salt
1 tablespoon vinegar
3 tablespoons butter
1½ cups mushrooms, sliced
2 tablespoons flour
5 cups veal or chicken stock
2 egg yolks
½ cup light cream
freshly ground black pepper

Wash the brains well, remove the thin membrane with a sharp knife, wash once more to remove any blood. Soak in cold water for 30 minutes. Put the brains into a saucepan with the salt and vinegar and add sufficient water to cover. Bring to boiling point. Reduce the heat, cover and simmer gently for 5 minutes. Rub through a strainer or purée in an electric blender. Heat the butter and sauté the mushrooms gently. Stir in the flour and add the stock gradually. Add the puréed brains. Stir the egg yolks with the cream and add half a cup of the hot broth. Return to the hot soup stirring constantly. Heat the soup until hot.

59

Prague Potato Soup

5 medium sized potatoes, peeled and diced
6 cups chicken stock
2 cups soup vegetables, (e.g. leek, onion, carrot, celery etc.) chopped
½ teaspoon caraway seeds
½ teaspoon marjoram
4 tablespoons butter
1 onion, chopped
1 clove garlic, chopped
2 tablespoons flour
1 cup mushrooms, sliced
1 egg yolk
½ cup light cream
1 teaspoon salt
freshly ground black pepper

Boil the potatoes for 20 minutes in the stock with the vegetables, caraway seeds and marjoram. Heat the butter and sauté the remaining onion and garlic until transluscent. Stir in the flour and cook for 2 minutes. Strain the soup and reserve some of the vegetables and potatoes for garnishing. Rub the remaining vegetables, with a little stock through a strainer or purée in an electric blender. Return the strained broth and puréed vegetables to the pot. Add the onion and garlic and simmer for 5 minutes. Add the reserved potatoes and vegetables together with the sliced mushrooms and simmer for another 5 minutes. Stir the egg yolk into the cream. Add a little of the hot broth and return this mixture to the soup. Heat until hot. Season with salt and pepper.

Polish Borsht

2 tablespoons butter
2 tablespoons oil
2 carrots, shredded
3 beets, shredded
1 onion, finely chopped
1 leek or additional onion, finely chopped
5 cups water
3 chicken bouillon cubes
6 slices bacon, cooked until crisp and crumbled
1 tablespoon finely chopped parsley
1 tablespoon finely chopped celery tops
1 teaspoon salt
freshly ground pepper
½ cup cooked chicken, game or duck, optional
1 fennel bulb cooked and diced, optional

This soup is as popular in Poland and Hungary as it is in Russia.
Heat the butter and oil and sauté the vegetables for 5 minutes. Add the water and bouillon cubes and simmer for 25 minutes. Add the bacon and the remaining ingredients. Heat until hot. Season with salt and pepper and garnish with the chicken, game or duck and fennel, if used.

Prague Potato Soup

Polish Borsht

Chanterelle Soup

4 tablespoons butter or suet
2 onions, finely chopped
2 teaspoons paprika
2 cups canned chanterelles
(these are woodland mushrooms found in Hungary and France, 4 ounced dried Polish mushrooms may be substituted)
5 cups chicken stock
½ cup sour cream
1 tablespoon flour
2 tablespoons finely chopped parsley
¼ cup heavy cream

Heat the butter or suet and sauté the onions for 3 minutes. Add the paprika. Add the drained chanterelles (or soaked dried mushrooms). Stir in the stock and bring to the boil. Blend the sour cream with the flour and stir into the soup. Simmer gently for 10 minutes and stir in the parsley and cream just before serving.

Austrian Oatmeal Soup

4 tablespoons butter
1 cup regular oatmeal, not instant
5 cups veal or chicken stock
1 teaspoon salt
freshly ground black pepper
⅛ teaspoon nutmeg
2 egg yolks
2 tablespoons finely chopped parsley

Heat the butter and sauté the oatmeal for 4 minutes, stirring constantly until golden brown. Add the stock and simmer gently for 20 minutes. Season with salt and pepper. Add the nutmeg. Beat the egg yolks lightly and stir in a little of the hot soup. Return to the saucepan and heat until hot but do not allow to boil. Garnish with parsley.

Austrian Leafy Green Soup

3 tablespoons butter
3 cups assorted spring greens such as young nettles, strawberry and currant leaves, watercress, pansy and dandelion greens, spinach etc. trimmed and finely chopped
8 cups water
4 chicken bouillon cubes
2 egg yolks
1 cup light cream
3 tablespoons flour
1 teaspoon salt
freshly ground black pepper
2 tablespoons finely chopped parsley
1 tablespoon finely chopped chives
2 cups croutons

The spring herbs and vegetables that go into this soup abound in Vienna just waiting to be picked. If you are not blessed with a garden, substitute tender young lettuce leaves and any other greenery you can find.

Heat the butter and sauté the green leaves for 2 minutes until wilted. Stir in the water and bouillon cubes. Simmer for 15 minutes and rub through a strainer or purée in an electric blender. Stir the egg yolks with the cream and flour and add to the soup. Season with salt and pepper. Heat until hot and garnish with parsley and chives. Serve with croutons.

Polish Beer Soup

4 cups beer
1 tablespoon cornstarch
2 tablespoons cold water
3 tablespoons butter
2 egg yolks
$\frac{1}{2}$ cup sour cream
$\frac{1}{3}$ cup cheese, grated
2 tablespoons finely chopped parsley
4 rounds white bread, toasted

Bring the beer to boiling point. Combine the cornstarch with the water and stir into the beer. Simmer gently for 3 minutes until the beer has thickened slightly. Stir in the butter. Stir the egg yolks with the sour cream and add to the soup. Serve the soup garnished with grated cheese and parsley. Float a round of toasted bread in each bowl.

Bouillon with Cheese Dumplings
Käsenockerln

3 tablespoons butter
2 eggs
3 tablespoons breadcrumbs
2 tablespoons chopped parsley
3 tablespoons cheese, grated
4 cups chicken stock

Beat the butter until soft and creamy. Add the eggs, breadcrumbs, parsley and cheese. Bring the stock to boiling point and reduce to simmer. With two moistened teaspoons, form the mixture into dumplings and add to the stock. Cover and simmer for 5 minutes until the dumplings float to the top of the broth.

Chlodnik

$\frac{3}{4}$ pound fresh beets
1 pound spinach
1 tablespoon sugar
1 cucumber, peeled, seeded and diced
3 hard-boiled eggs, chopped
$\frac{1}{2}$ pound shrimp, cooked, shelled, deveined and chopped
juice of 1 lemon
2 tablespoons finely chopped dill
3 tablespoons finely chopped chives
4 cups yogurt
2 cups beer
1 teaspoon salt
freshly ground black pepper
$\frac{1}{4}$ pound whole small shrimp for garnish

There are many variations of this cold soup. In Warsaw for example, sorrel is sometimes substituted for the shrimp and stock replaces the beer.

Cook the beets in sufficient cold water to cover for 30 minutes until soft. Peel and dice the beets. Wash the spinach and cook for 3 minutes in a covered pan with only the water clinging to the leaves. Add the spinach to the beets. Add the sugar and all the remaining ingredients except the garnishing shrimps. Combine all the ingredients and chill for 2 hours. Garnish with the reserved shrimps.

The Balkan Countries

Greece is justly proud of its fish soups and all her many other fish dishes, yet Avgolemono, that delightful blend of chicken stock, lemon juice and egg, is its national soup. Greek cooking without lemon would be as unthinkable as without herbs. The many years of Turkish domination have left their mark on the Greek cuisine so that often it is difficult to tell whether a certain dish is of Greek or Turkish origin. The eggplant might well be dubbed Rumania's national vegetable, and Rumanian cooks have created a wealth of dishes in its honor. It almost seems as though every other Rumanian has a favorite eggplant recipe. The country's national soup is the Ciorba, a vegetable soup with meatballs. In addition to eggplant, ciorba and the variety of other good things, Rumanians love meatballs, sweet desserts, jams and crystallized fruits.

The Yugoslav cuisine reflects the many different influences that have helped shape its national life and vary from Croatian and Slovakian to Serbian, Bosnian and Macedonian. All have their regional specialties and favorite dishes and all start the most important meal of the day with soup.

Greek Lentil Soup

1 pound lentils
8 cups water
16 ounce can Italian plum tomatoes
⅓ cup olive oil
5 chicken bouillon cubes
3 cloves garlic, peeled
1 teaspoon oregano
1 bay leaf
peel of 1 orange
3 fresh tomatoes, peeled, seeded and chopped
1 teaspoon salt
freshly ground black pepper

Soak the lentils for 12 hours in the water. Bring to simmering point. Cover and simmer for 2 hours. Add all the remaining ingredients. Discard the bay leaf, orange peel and garlic. Simmer for 10 minutes and serve piping hot.

Rumanian Chicken Soup

3 tablespoons olive oil
1 green pepper, seeded and chopped
1 small eggplant, diced
⅛ teaspoon cayenne pepper
½ teaspoon oregano
½ teaspoon rosemary
1½ tablespoons flour
2 tablespoons lemon juice
5 cups chicken stock
1 cup cooked chicken, diced
1 teaspoon salt
freshly ground black pepper
1 egg yolk
½ cup light cream

Heat the oil and sauté the pepper and eggplant for 5 minutes. Add the cayenne pepper, oregano and rosemary. Stir in the flour and add the lemon juice. Add the chicken stock gradually. Simmer for 10 minutes. Add the chicken and season with salt and pepper. Stir the egg yolk with the cream and stir in a little of the hot broth. Return to the saucepan and heat until hot.

Greek White Bean and Tomato Soup

1 pound dried white beans
8 cups water
2 teaspoons salt
⅓ cup olive oil
4 onions, finely chopped
4 stalks celery, thinly sliced
2 tablespoons tomato paste
3 medium sized tomatoes, peeled, seeded and chopped
1 teaspoon thyme
½ teaspoon marjoram
1 tablespoon vinegar
1 tablespoon sugar
freshly ground black pepper
2 tablespoons finely chopped parsley

Soak the beans in the water. Add the salt and bring to boiling point. Reduce the heat. Cover and simmer for 2 hours. Heat the oil and sauté the onions and celery for 5 minutes. Add the tomato paste, chopped tomatoes, thyme, marjoram, vinegar and sugar. Simmer for 15 minutes. Stir this mixture into the bean soup. Season with pepper and simmer for 15 more minutes. Garnish with chopped parsley.

Transylvanian Peasant Soup

2 tablespoons oil
1 onion, finely chopped
2 teaspoons paprika
1 pound lean beef, cut into
small pieces
½ pound calf's liver, cut into
small pieces
3 tablespoons flour
1 cup red wine
1 teaspoon salt
4 cups water
3 beef bouillon cubes
1 red or green pepper, seeded
and diced
3 medium sized potatoes,
peeled and diced
2 tablespoons finely chopped
chives

Heat the oil and sauté the onion for 3 minutes. Add the paprika and sauté the beef and liver until lightly colored on all sides. Stir in the flour and add the wine. Season with salt and stir in the water. Add the bouillon cubes and simmer for 30 minutes. Add the green or red pepper and potatoes. Cover and simmer for 20 minutes. Garnish with chopped chives.

Greek Vegetable Soup

⅓ cup olive oil
1 onion, finely chopped
4 ripe tomatoes, peeled, seeded
and chopped
4 cups cabbage, shredded
8 cups chicken stock
1 teaspoon salt
freshly ground black pepper
¼ cup uncooked rice
1 cup cooked chicken, diced
juice of 2 lemons
2 egg yolks
½ cup light cream

Heat the oil and sauté the onion for 5 minutes until golden. Add the tomatoes, cabbage, chicken stock, salt, pepper and rice and simmer gently for 20 minutes. Stir in the chicken and lemon juice and simmer for 5 more minutes. Stir the egg yolks with the cream and stir into the hot soup. Heat until hot but do not allow to boil.

Bulgarian Lamb Soup

½ pound stewing lamb, cut into
small pieces
6 cups simmering beef stock
3 green peppers, seeded and
chopped
1 onion, finely chopped
¼ cup uncooked rice
grated rind and juice of 1 lemon
3 tablespoons butter
3 tablespoons flour
2 tablespoons tomato paste
2 egg yolks
½ cup plain yogurt
freshly ground black pepper
2 tablespoons finely chopped
parsley

Simmer the lamb in the beef stock for 40 minutes until almost cooked. Add the peppers, onion, rice, grated lemon rind and juice and simmer for 15 minutes. Heat the butter and stir in the flour. Add the tomato paste and add this mixture to the soup. Stir for 5 minutes until thickened slightly. Stir the egg yolks into the yogurt and add to the hot soup. Season with pepper and garnish with parsley.

Croatian Fish Soup

6 cups water
1 onion, sliced
2 cloves garlic, peeled
2 teaspoons salt
4 peppercorns
1 tablespoon vinegar
1 teaspoon rosemary
2 pound fish i.e. cod, haddock,
bass, etc. cut into bite
sized pieces
¼ cup uncooked rice
1 tablespoon tomato paste
juice of 1 lemon
2 tablespoons finely chopped
parsley

The fishermen along the Croatian coast cook the fish in fresh seawater with plenty of ripe tomatoes and serve it with the hard Yugoslav bread known as Kolac or Baskot.

Boil the water with the onion, garlic, salt, peppercorns, vinegar and rosemary for 15 minutes. Add the fish and simmer for 8 minutes until tender. Remove the fish from the stock with a slotted spoon and keep it warm. Strain the stock and add the rice. Cover and cook gently for 20 minutes. Stir in the tomato paste, lemon juice and parsley. Put the fish into warmed bowls and fill the bowls with piping hot soup.

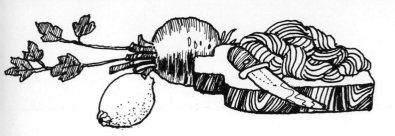

Tarator

2 large or 3 small cucumbers, thinly sliced

2 teaspoons salt

2 cups yogurt

freshly ground black pepper

1 clove garlic, finely chopped

½ cup walnuts, chopped

Yogurt is a Balkan specialty and along with bread, onions and olives, one of its most important foods. The Balkan peoples are noted for their longevity and they tend to attribute their long life and good health to their prodigious consumption of yogurt. This cold Tarator soup is an example of the role of yogurt in the daily diet.

Put the sliced cucumbers into a bowl. Add the salt and chill for 1 hour. Drain and rinse the cucumber and pat dry on paper towels. Fold in the yogurt and season with pepper. Add the garlic. Serve the soup in bowls sprinkled with chopped walnuts.

Rumanian Soup with Meatballs
Ciora

8 cups beef stock

juice of 4 lemons or 1 cup sauerkraut juice

¼ cup uncooked rice

¼ pound ground veal

¼ pound ground pork

1 egg

1 teaspoon salt

freshly ground black pepper

2 tablespoons finely chopped parsley

¼ cup chopped onion

½ teaspoon thyme

1 teaspoon flour

1 stalk celery, finely chopped

3 leeks or 2 onions, thinly sliced

½ fennel bulb, optional

½ teaspoon thyme

3 sprigs parsley

½ teaspoon tarragon

⅛ teaspoon cayenne pepper

2 egg yolks

½ cup sour cream

1 tablespoon cornstarch

2 tablespoons finely chopped dill,

chives or tarragon

Ciorba, Rumania's national soup, can be prepared in a variety of ways. Chicken or lamb stock may be substituted for the beef stock, and red beets are often added. It is a pungent soup and like so many soups it can be served as a main course. The flavor will improve if it is made a day or two in advance.

Bring the stock to the boil. Add the lemon juice and rice. Mix the ground veal and pork with the egg and season with salt and pepper. Add the parsley, onion and thyme and shape into small balls. Dust with flour and add to the soup together with the celery, leeks, fennel, thyme, parsley, tarragon and cayenne pepper. Simmer for 15 minutes. Stir the egg yolks into the sour cream. Stir in the cornstarch. Add a little cold water to make a thin paste and stir this mixture into the soup. Simmer but do not boil for 20 minutes. Taste the broth and if it is too sharp, add a little water and a teaspoon of sugar. If it is not sufficiently pungent, add a little more lemon juice or sauerkraut juice. Serve the soup garnished with a spoonful of sour cream topped with dill chives, or tarragon.

Bulgarian Soup with Dumplings

2 cups flour

2 eggs

¼ teaspoon salt

1 tablespoon rendered beef fat or butter

5 cups chicken stock

⅛ teaspoon nutmeg

2 tablespoons finely chopped chives

Mix the flour with the eggs, salt and rendered beef fat or butter. Add a little lukewarm water if necessary to soften the dough. Form into small dumplings. Bring the stock to boiling point and reduce to simmer. Add the dumplings and nutmeg and simmer for 10 minutes until they rise to the surface of the stock. Sprinkle with chopped chives.

Serbian Spinach Soup

1 pound spinach, heavy stems removed and washed
5 cups water
3 chicken bouillon cubes
½ cup bacon, diced
3 tablespoons butter
1 onion, chopped
1 clove garlic, finely chopped
3 tablespoons flour
1 teaspoon salt
freshly ground black pepper
1 egg yolk
½ cup light cream

Boil the spinach in the water with the bouillon cubes for 3 minutes until tender. Rub through a strainer or purée in an electric blender. Cook the bacon until all the fat has rendered and leave to one side. Heat the butter and sauté the onion and garlic for 3 minutes. Stir in the flour and add to the soup with the bacon. Season with salt and pepper. Stir the egg yolk into the cream and add to the soup. Stir until hot but do not allow to boil.

Mushroom and Potato Soup

2 tablespoons oil
3 cloves garlic, finely chopped
1 pound mushrooms, sliced
1 tablespoon flour
5 cups water
3 chicken bouillon cubes
2 ripe tomatoes, peeled, seeded and chopped
1 teaspoon salt
freshly ground black pepper
¼ cup sour cream
2 tablespoons finely chopped parsley

Heat the oil and sauté the garlic for 2 minutes until lightly browned. Add the mushrooms and cook gently for 3 minutes. Stir in the flour and add the water gradually. Add the bouillon cubes and tomatoes. Simmer the soup for 25 minutes. Season with salt and pepper and stir in the sour cream and parsley just before serving.

Greek Egg and Lemon Soup
Avgolemono

½ cup uncooked rice
1 teaspoon salt
5 cups chicken stock
4 eggs
juice of 2 lemons

This is the national soup of Greece, beloved by natives and tourists alike. Cook the rice in the salted stock for 20 minutes until the rice is tender. Beat the eggs until light and fluffy and stir in the lemon juice, drop by drop. While still stirring add a little of the hot broth and stir this mixture back into the soup. Take great care not to let the soup regain the boil or the eggs will scramble. Serve immediately.

Meatless Borsht

1 pound beets, boiled, peeled and grated
5 cups chicken stock
1 onion, finely chopped
3 carrots, grated
3 cups cabbage, shredded
1 tablespoon lemon juice or vinegar
⅓ cup sour cream

Combine the beets, chicken stock, onion, carrots and cabbage in a large saucepan. Cover and simmer for 20 minutes. Add the lemon juice or vinegar and ladle into soup bowls. Garnish with a spoonful of sour cream.

Eastern Europe

According to local lore, Ivan the Terrible, who ruled Russia with an iron hand during the sixteenth century could be placated with only one thing - a cup of good borsht. A hundred years later Catharine II arrived with some of her French cooks and the cooking of Russia took a decidedly more sophisticated turn. Catharine had, however, much in common with Ivan the Terrible. Both esteemed soup above all other foods. Catharine was the more sociable of the two rulers and she liked to share her supper with Prince Potemkin. During one of these meals, Catharine let the word slip that there was nothing that would please her more than a drop of sturgeon soup. Such a word was a command but alas, not a single sturgeon was to be found throughout the markets of Moscow. Potemkin's servants combed the city and eventually came across a wealthy merchant who had by now heard news of Potemkin's dilemma. He offered to trade Potemkin a sturgeon for a Del Sarto Madonna. Though the prince had paid more than 10,000 rubles for the painting, he had no choice but to accept the terms of the bargain. Thus Catherine dined on the most expensive soup in history and Potemkin kept his head long enough to taste it with her.

Cold Turkish Yogurt Soup

grated rind and juice of 1 lemon
2 cucumbers, peeled and grated
1 teaspoon finely chopped dillweed
1 clove garlic, finely chopped
3 tablespoons oil
1 teaspoon dill seed
1 tablespoon finely chopped mint leaves
4 cups plain yogurt

Combine all the ingredients and chill for 4 hours. Pour off the liquid that will form at the sides of the bowl.

Borsht with Meat

1½ pounds beets, boiled, peeled and grated
2 tablespoons vinegar
1 teaspoon sugar
1 pound lean beef
8 cups water
½ pound lean bacon
1 tablespoon salt
8 peppercorns
6 sprigs parsley
2 teaspoons marjoram
2 teaspoons dill seed or basil
2 leeks or 1 extra onion, thinly sliced
1 onion, finely chopped
1 carrot, grated
1 pound cabbage, grated
1 Polish sausage
2 tablespoons finely chopped dill, chives or parsley
1 cup sour cream

There must be as many borsht recipes as there are spellings of the name, but whatever the recipe and regardless of whether it is served hot or cold, the main ingredient of borsht is the beet. The soup may be served garnished with sweet or sour cream and it can be made with fish, meat, kidneys, bacon, ham, sausage, duck, mushrooms, dried fruit or vegetables.

Peel and grate two of the beets and marinate overnight in the vinegar and sugar. Simmer the beef gently in the water for 2 hours together with the bacon, salt, peppercorns, parsley, marjoram and dill seed. Discard the parsley. Add the remaining beets with the leeks, onion, carrot, cabbage and sausage and simmer for another 30 minutes. Remove the beef, bacon and sausage from the soup. Cut into small pieces and return to the pot. Stir the drained marinated beets into the soup. To serve, sprinkle with the chopped herbs and garnish each serving with a generous spoonful of sour cream.

Russian Vegetable Soup with Stuffed Cabbage Rolls

1 large potato, peeled and diced
1 carrot, sliced
1 onion, finely chopped
4 stalks celery, sliced
4 sprigs parsley
5 cups water
5 chicken bouillon cubes
4 large cabbage leaves
½ cup ground veal
1 slice bread soaked in
2 tablespoons cold water
1 egg
1 teaspoon salt
freshly ground black pepper
½ teaspoon marjoram
½ teaspoon thyme
1 tomato, peeled, seeded and chopped
1 cup canned corn
½ cup hard cheese, grated

Cook the potato, carrot, onion, celery and parsley in the water together with the bouillon cubes for 20 minutes. Meanwhile, parboil the cabbage leaves in salted water for 10 minutes, pat dry and flatten them. Mix the ground veal with the bread, egg, salt, pepper, marjoram and thyme. Divide the mixture between the 4 leaves and roll securely, tucking the ends in to form neat packages. Place the cabbage rolls in an ovenproof dish. Pour the soup over them and top with the tomato and drained corn. Sprinkle with grated cheese and cook in a preheated 350° oven for 40 minutes. Place under the broiler for 3 minutes to brown the cheese.

Russian Beef Tongue and Vegetable Soup

2 pound whole pickled beef tongue
5 cups water
3 carrots, grated
2 onions, finely chopped
2 leeks or one additional onion, chopped
2 stalks celery, sliced
3 sprigs parsley
1 bay leaf
1 teaspoon thyme
½ teaspoon basil
8 peppercorns
1 tablespoon salt
1 cup mushrooms, finely chopped
2 tablespoons finely chopped parsley
½ cup light cream

Tongue has to be boiled, and the cooking liquid makes a fine base for soups. This vegetable soup recipe uses the tongue stock as its base. Once cooked, tongue, can be cut into thin strips and served in the soup or sliced and served separately with bread.

Soak the tongue for 12 hours in cold water and rinse under running water. Put the tongue into a large saucepan and add the water, carrots, onions, leeks, celery, parsley, bay leaf, thyme, basil, peppercorns and salt. Cover and simmer gently for 3 hours. Discard the bay leaf and carefully lift the tongue out of the soup. Peel the tongue and discard any fatty tissue. Cool the soup and skim off all the fat. Rub the soup through a strainer or purée in an electric blender. Return to boiling point and add the mushrooms. Simmer for 10 minutes. Season to taste and stir in the parsley and cream.

If the tongue is to be served with the soup, slice and cut it into thin strips. Save the remaining tongue for another meal.

Turkish Lamb Soup with Tomatoes

1 pound stewing lamb
8 cups lukewarm water
4 tomatoes, peeled, seeded and chopped
5 onions, peeled and sliced
¾ cup dried apricots, chopped
1 bay leaf
½ teaspoon thyme
½ teaspoon marjoram
4 peppercorns
1 teaspoon salt
¼ pound thin noodles
freshly ground black pepper
2 tablespoons finely chopped parsley

The dried apricots give this soup a sweet yet somewhat tart flavor.

Put the lamb into a large saucepan and add the water, tomatoes, onions and apricots. Bring to the boil, add the bay leaf, thyme, marjoram, peppercorns and salt. Cover and simmer gently for 2 hours until the apricots disintegrate and the lamb is very tender. During the last 10 minutes, lift the lamb from the soup and add the noodles. Cut the lamb into small pieces and return it to the soup. Season with salt and pepper and garnish with parsley.

Turkish Chicken Soup
Tavuk Corbasi

2 tablespoons uncooked rice
½ teaspoon tarragon
8 cups chicken stock
3 tablespoons butter
3 tablespoons flour
I cup yogurt
I teaspoon salt
freshly ground black pepper
I cup cooked chicken, diced
I teaspoon grated lemon rind
I tablespoon lemon juice
2 tablespoons finely chopped chives

Cook the rice with the tarragon in the stock for 20 minutes until tender. Heat the butter. Stir in the flour and add the yogurt. Cook over a very low heat, do not allow the yogurt to become too hot or it will curdle. Season with salt and pepper and add the remaining ingredients.

Schi

I pound sauerkraut
½ pound stewing beef, cut into small pieces
8 cups beef stock
4 tablespoons butter
2 onions, finely chopped
2 carrots sliced
4 tablespoons flour
I tablespoon tomato paste
½ teaspoon thyme
½ teaspoon basil
¼ teaspoon caraway seeds
I teaspoon salt
freshly ground black pepper
I cup sour cream
tablespoons chopped dillweed

This traditional Russian soup is almost as popular as borsht and there are many ways of preparing it. It is usually made with sauerkraut, but plain cabbage, spinach or sorrel may be substituted. Fish or eggs may be used to replace the beef. The soup is invariably served with sour cream and accompanied by cheese, meat or cabbage filled pastries.
Cook the sauerkraut and beef in the stock for I½ hours until tender. Heat the butter and sauté the onions and carrots for 5 minutes. Stir in the flour. Add the tomato paste, thyme, basil and caraway seeds. Add the mixture to the soup and stir until it has thickened slightly. Simmer for another 30 minutes. Season with salt and pepper. Serve into soup bowls and top each bowl with sour cream and sprinkle with dillweed.

Strawberry Soup

I pint strawberries, washed and hulled
2 cups carbonated water
3 egg yolks
½ cup sugar
I cup heavy cream
I pint vanilla ice cream
4 orange sections
4 grapefruit sections
4 whole strawberries

This is a dessert soup and usually served with thin wafers.
Soak the strawberries in the carbonated water. In the top of a double boiler, beat the egg yolks with the sugar until thick and add the cream. Stir over boiling water until the soup thickens into the consistency of a light custard. Cool and stir from time to time to prevent a skin from forming. Rub the strawberries through a strainer or purée in an electric blender and stir into the cooled custard. Ladle into deep bowls and add a spoonful of ice cream to each bowl. Garnish with the orange and grapefruit sections and whole strawberries.

Russian Wine Soup

2 cups dry white wine
2 cups water
⅓ cup sugar
4 thin slices lemon
I cinnamon stick
I tablespoon arrowroot or cornstarch dissolved in
2 tablespoons cold water
3 egg yolks
¼ cup vodka
baked meringues

This soup can be served hot or cold either as a first course or as a dessert.
Combine the wine, water, sugar, lemon and cinnamon stick in a saucepan and bring to the boil. Dissolve the arrowroot or cornstarch in the cold water and stir into the wine broth. Stir the egg yolks into the vodka. Add a few spoonfuls of the hot broth and stir the mixture into the soup. Do not allow to boil. Serve with tiny meringues.

Turkish Mutton Soup
Ekshili ts chorbo

¾ pound mutton or lamb, in one piece
5 cups water
2 leeks, or 1 additional onion, sliced
1 onion, sliced
3 carrots
3 stalks celery, sliced
4 sprigs parsley
1 teaspoon thyme
3 tablespoons oil
1 tablespoon flour
1 teaspoon salt
freshly grated black pepper
juice of 1 lemon
1 teaspoon sugar
4 egg yolks
½ teaspoon chervil

Simmer the mutton or lamb for 1½ hours in the water. Add the vegetables, parsley and thyme and simmer for another 20 minutes. Heat the oil and stir in the flour. Add to the soup. Discard the parsley. Season with salt, pepper, lemon juice and sugar.

Remove the meat from the broth. Slice and keep it warm. Put 1 egg yolk into each bowl. Pour the soup over the yolk and stir well. Garnish with chopped chervil. Serve the meat separately with bread.

Rassolnik

2 veal kidneys (approximately 1 pound)
5 cups water
1 teaspoon salt
2 small cucumbers, peeled, seeded and chopped
2 onions, chopped
3 tablespoons butter
3 tablespoons flour
½ cup spinach, finely chopped
1 teaspoon salt, if necessary
freshly ground black pepper
2 hard-boiled eggs, finely chopped
2 tablespoons finely chopped parsley

One of the lesser-known adventures of the notorious Baron von Munchhausen has to do with the delicious Russian kidney soup called Rassolnik. It seems that Munchhausen travelled to Smolensk in 1765 for the sole purpose of winning a bet he had made, namely, that he could consume a thousand plates of Rassolnik, no mean feat! He apparently won the bet and collected his winnings of 1,000 gold rubles. Sadly, though, it is rumoured that he was never quite the same again.

To prepare this soup, bring the kidneys to the boil in sufficient cold water to cover. Drain and rinse them under cold water. Return to the saucepan with 5 cups of water and salt and simmer gently for 45 minutes. Chop the kidneys and reserve. Sauté the cucumbers and onions in the butter for 5 minutes. Sprinkle with flour and add the kidney stock gradually. Simmer the soup gently for 15 minutes. Add the chopped kidneys and spinach. Season with salt and pepper and garnish with chopped egg and parsley.

Turkish Mutton Soup

New Delhi Soup

New Delhi Soup

2 tablespoons oil	Heat the oil and sauté the peppers and
2 green peppers, seeded and chopped	onions for 5 minutes. Stir in the curry powder and flour. Add the tomato paste.
2 onions, finely chopped	Stir in the water and bouillon cubes and
1 tablespoon curry powder	simmer gently for 15 minutes. Add the
1 tablespoon flour	cream.
2 tablespoons tomato paste	
4 cups water	
4 chicken bouillon cubes	
½ cup light cream	

The Middle East

Onion soup is a typically French dish, or so the French tell us. However, it would seem that onion soup was being cooked in Persia, a country famous for its delicate soups, long before the reign of Julius Caesar. The recipe of the 'original' onion soup as well as other regional specialties form a part of this chapter.

In India, soup is generally served after the main curry course and immediately before the dessert.

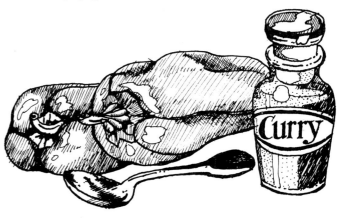

Indian Curry Soup with Meat Balls

3 tablespoons butter
2 teaspoons curry powder
2 tablespoons flour
5 cups beef stock
¼ pound ground beef
1 small onion, finely chopped
1 teaspoon curry powder
½ teaspoon salt
freshly ground black pepper
½ cup thin noodles
½ teaspoon dried mint
2 tablespoons finely chopped parsley

Heat the butter and stir in the curry powder and flour. Add the beef stock and simmer for 5 minutes. Mix the ground beef with the onion, curry powder, salt and pepper and form into small meatballs. Drop these into the soup. Add the noodles and simmer gently for 10 minutes until the meatballs rise to the surface of the stock. Add the dried mint and garnish with parsley.

Dahl Soup

½ cup lentils
8 cups water
1 teaspoon salt
2 onions, finely chopped
1 green pepper, seeded and chopped
1 clove garlic, finely chopped
3 tablespoons curry powder
3 tablespoons butter or
4 tablespoons oil
1 teaspoon lemon juice

The Indian dahl soup is very similar to European lentil soup.
Soak the lentils in the water overnight. Bring to simmering point. Cover and cook over low heat for 1 hour. Add the salt. Sauté the onions, green pepper, garlic and curry powder in the butter or oil for 10 minutes. Stir the mixture into the soup. Add the lemon juice and simmer for 10 minutes.

Pomegranate Soup

¼ pound ground veal
1 slice white bread, made into breadcrumbs
2 tablespoons cold water
½ small onion, finely chopped
1 teaspoon salt
freshly ground black pepper
½ teaspoon cinnamon
½ cup cooked rice
6 cups hot beef stock
juice 1 pomegranate
1 small onion, finely chopped
1 cup spinach, chopped
1 teaspoon sugar
1 teaspoon lemon juice
2 tablespoons finely chopped parsley

Mix the ground veal with the breadcrumbs, water, onion, salt, pepper and cinnamon and form into small meatballs. Add the rice to the hot stock. In an electric juice extractor, obtain the juice from the pomegranate flesh and seeds. Strain the juice and add to the hot stock. Add the onion, spinach, sugar and meatballs. Simmer for 15 minutes. Add the lemon juice and garnish with parsley.

Persian Vegetable Soup
Ache-e-sac

½ pound yellow split peas
8 cups water
1 pound mutton or lamb, ground
2 tablespoons rice flour or cornstarch
1½ teaspoons cinnamon
1 teaspoon salt
freshly ground black pepper
1 pound spinach, stems removed and chopped
juice 1 lemon
1 tablespoon finely chopped fresh mint or 1 teaspoon dried mint

Soak the peas overnight in the water. Bring to boiling point. Cover and simmer for 1 hour. Mix the ground mutton or lamb with the rice flour or cornstarch, cinnamon, salt and pepper. Form into small meatballs and add to the soup. Simmer for 30 minutes. Add the spinach, lemon juice and mint and simmer for 10 minutes.

Persian Barley Soup

¼ cup barley
1 teaspoon salt
1½ cups water
2 tablespoons butter
2 onions, finely chopped
5 cups beef or chicken stock
2 medium sized tomatoes, peeled, seeded and chopped
⅓ teaspoon salt
freshly ground black pepper

Simmer the barley for 30 minutes in the salted water and drain. Heat the butter and sauté the onions for 5 minutes. Add the stock to the onions and simmer for 10 minutes. Add the tomatoes and barley and simmer for another 10 minutes. Season with salt and pepper.

Persian Prune Soup

1 cup pitted prunes
1 pound spinach, stems removed and chopped
1 large onion, finely chopped
1 cucumber, peeled, seeded and chopped
¼ cup uncooked rice
½ cup lentils
8 cups water
6 chicken bouillon cubes
1 teaspoon salt
freshly ground black pepper
2 tablespoons finely chopped parsley

The people of Iran firmly believe that this soup is a cure for the common cold. Put all the ingredients except the salt, pepper and parsley into a large saucepan. Cover and simmer gently for 2 hours until the prunes and the vegetables are tender. Season to taste with salt and pepper and garnish with parsley.

Mulligatawny Soup

1 pound lentils
10 cups water
2 chickens each weighing approximately 2¼ pounds, quartered
2 teaspoons salt
3 bay leaves
¼ cup oil
2 onions, finely chopped
3–4 tablespoons curry powder
4 cloves garlic, finely chopped
⅛ teaspoon cayenne pepper
⅓ cup grated coconut
¼ cup rice flour
1 cup rice
1 sliced lemon

Mulligatawny soup originated in southern India. In the Tamil language of that region, Mulligatawny means pepper water.
The rice served with this golden soup should be presented separately and spooned into the individual bowls at the table. It is an ideal soup for an informal gathering and can be served as a main course preceded by a salad and followed by ice cream.
Soak the lentils in the water for 2 hours. Add the chickens and sufficient cold water to cover. Add the salt and bay leaves. Cover and simmer for 1 hour. Take the chickens from the soup and discard the bay leaves. Rub the lentils through a strainer or purée in an electric blender. Discard the chicken skin and bones and cut the meat into small pieces. Heat the oil and sauté the onions with the curry powder, garlic, cayenne pepper and coconut. Stir in the flour and add to the soup stirring constantly. Simmer gently for 15 minutes. Add the chicken meat and season with more salt and cayenne pepper if necessary. Meanwhile boil the rice and serve separately. Place a slice of lemon in each soup bowl and add the hot soup.

Cold Cucumber Soup
Doogh Khiar

1 cucumber, peeled, seeded and chopped
1 onion, finely chopped
2 cups yogurt
1 teaspoon fresh mint or ½ teaspoon dried mint
1 teaspoon basil
¼ cup finely chopped nuts, e.g. walnuts, filberts or almonds
¼ cup raisins, soaked in hot water for 5 minutes and drained
1 teaspoon salt
2 cups chilled chicken stock

Stir all the ingredients except the chicken stock together. Chill for 4 hours. Stir in the chicken stock just before serving.

Persian Onion Soup

4 tablespoons oil
4 medium sized onions sliced
1 tablespoon curry powder
3 tablespoons flour
6 cups water
5 chicken or beef bouillon cubes
1 tablespoon lemon juice
1 tablespoon finely chopped
fresh mint or 1 teaspoon dried
mint
1 teaspoon cinnamon
1 teaspoon salt
freshly ground black pepper
2 egg yolks

Heat the oil and sauté the onions and curry for 5 minutes. Stir in the flour and add the water gradually. Add the bouillon cubes and simmer for 30 minutes. Add the lemon juice, mint and cinnamon and simmer for another 10 minutes. Season with salt and pepper. Beat the egg yolks until light and frothy and stir in a little of the hot soup. Add the mixture to the soup in the saucepan and heat until hot but do not allow to boil.

The Far East

Chinese cooking is to be found in every corner of the world and there are very few capital cities that do not boast of at least one Chinese restaurant. Among the masterful creations of the Chinese cuisine, the soups rank very highly. Some are sufficient for a whole meal and others are served instead of a beverage throughout the meal.

The Chinese cuisine can be roughly divided into three regional styles; those of Canton, Peking and Shanghai. All make use of many of the same basic ingredients including soy sauce, herbs, garlic, onion, ginger root, noodles, oil and rice wine. Milk, bread, butter, cream and cheese are virtually unknown. Sweet desserts are served on special occasions but are not part of the daily diet.

The Chinese cuisine has left its imprint on the cooking of many lands, not only in the Far East, but all over the world. Even the most sophisticated French cooking owes much to the utter simplicity, emphasis on fresh ingredients and exquisite presentations that are the hallmark of Chinese cooking.

Peking Pork Soup

¼ pound lean pork, cut into thin strips
2 tablespoons oil
2 cups Chinese cabbage, shredded
½ cup mushrooms, sliced
6 cups chicken stock
1 tablespoon dry sherry
1 thin slice fresh ginger root, minced
1 teaspoon salt
freshly ground black pepper
1 teaspoon cornstarch dissolved in 1 tablespoon cold water

Although beef is an integral part of Chinese cooking, it is not as widely used as pork. Veal is rare and lamb is used only in the north of China. Rice wine is a frequently used ingredient, but dry sherry may be substituted.

Sauté the pork in hot oil. Add the cabbage and mushrooms and sauté for 2 minutes. Stir in the stock, sherry, ginger root, salt and pepper. Simmer for 15 minutes until the cabbage is tender. Stir in the cornstarch dissolved in cold water and simmer for 2 minutes until the soup has thickened slightly.

Fish Soup with Pineapple

Fish Soup with Pineapple

1 pound fresh white fish fillets, cut into bite sized pieces
6 cups fish stock
1 teaspoon salt
1 tomato, peeled, seeded and chopped
4 slices fresh or canned pineapple, cut into small pieces
½ teaspoon basil
¼ teaspoon coriander
⅛ teaspoon cayenne pepper
2 tablespoons finely chopped cilantro or parsley
½ cup freshly boiled rice

Combine the fish, fish stock and salt and bring to simmering point. Add the tomato, pineapple, basil, coriander and cayenne pepper. Simmer gently for 6 minutes until the fish is barely tender. Just before serving, sprinkle with cilantro or parsley. Spoon the rice into the soup bowls at the table.

Clear Soup with Chicken Dumplings

1 cup ground raw chicken
4 scallions, very finely chopped
½ cup mushrooms, very finely chopped
1 thin slice fresh ginger root, minced
⅛ teaspoon cayenne pepper
1 egg
1 teaspoon salt
6 cups chicken stock
6 small clusters parsley

Combine the chicken with the scallions, mushrooms, ginger root, cayenne pepper, egg and salt and knead until firm. Form into tiny balls. Bring the stock to simmering point and poach the chicken dumplings for 5 minutes until they rise to the surface. Garnish the soup with parsley clusters.

Chinese Vegetable Soup with Shrimp

¼ pound shrimp, shelled, deveined and finely chopped
1 egg white, stiffly beaten
½ teaspoon salt
1 thin slice fresh ginger root, minced
6 cups chicken stock
2 tablespoons celery tops, finely chopped
1½ cups Chinese cabbage, finely chopped
1 tablespoon cornstarch dissolved in 2 tablespoons cold water
½ cup spinach, chopped
2 scallions, thinly sliced

In Chinese cooking it is important to assemble and prepare all the ingredients in advance because the preparation of many dishes involves the rapid assembly of many different ingredients and there must not be a moment lost once the cooking begins or the fresh quality and flavors are lost.

Stir the shrimp into the beaten egg white and add the salt and ginger root. Bring the stock to simmering point and add the celery tops and cabbage. Stir the cornstarch into the cold water. Simmer the soup for 15 minutes until the cabbage is tender. Stir in the cornstarch mixture. Add the shrimp mixture and simmer for 3 minutes. Add the spinach and scallions and cook for 1 minute longer. Serve immediately.

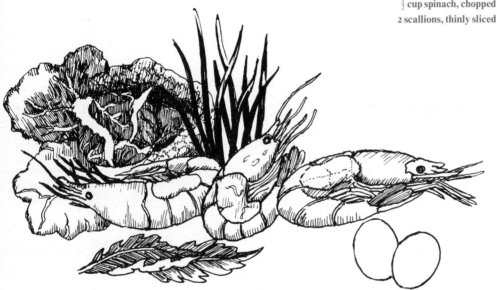

Chicken and Corn Soup

½ cup cooked chicken, diced
1 clove garlic, finely chopped
1 teaspoon salt
freshly ground black pepper
8 ounce can corn
5 cups chicken stock
1 egg yolk
1 tablespoon ham, finely chopped
2 tablespoons finely chopped parsley

Place the chicken in a bowl and add the garlic, salt, pepper and corn. Bring the stock to simmering point and add the chicken mixture. Reserve the liquid from the canned corn. Simmer for 5 minutes. Stir the egg yolk with the corn liquid and add to the hot soup. Heat until hot but do not allow to boil. Sprinkle with chopped ham and parsley.

Vietnamese Vegetable Soup with Shrimp
Canh Chua

½ pound jumbo shrimp, shelled and deveined
1 teaspoon salt
6 cups chicken stock
4 tomatoes, peeled, seeded and chopped
¼ pound fresh bean sprouts
½ teaspoon salt
freshly ground black pepper
8 finely chopped mint leaves

Split the shrimp along the backs with a sharp knife and sprinkle with salt. Bring the stock to boiling point. Add the shrimp, tomatoes and bean sprouts and season with salt and pepper. Serve the soup and garnish each bowl with freshly chopped mint leaves.

Thai Clear Soup with Fishballs

½ pound fresh flounder fillets, ground
1 teaspoon salt
freshly ground black pepper
6 cups fish stock
1 clove garlic, peeled
1 tablespoon soy sauce
¼ teaspoon coriander
¾ cup sliced mushrooms
¼ cup bean sprouts
2 tablespoons celery tops, finely chopped

Season the fish with salt and pepper and form into small balls. Bring the stock to boiling point. Reduce the heat to simmer and add the garlic, soy sauce and coriander. Add the mushrooms and simmer for 2 minutes. Add the fish balls and simmer for 6 minutes until they rise to the surface. Add the bean sprouts and celery tops and serve immediately.

Polynesian Chicken Soup with Noodles

1 pound chicken, cut into serving pieces
1 teaspoon salt
freshly ground black pepper
1 bay leaf
6 cups water
2 chicken bouillon cubes
¼ cup fine noodles
3 tablespoons butter
1 small onion, finely chopped
1 cup mushrooms, thinly sliced
½ teaspoon salt
freshly ground black pepper
2 tablespoons dry sherry
2 teaspoons lemon juice
½ teaspoon thyme

Simmer the chicken with the salt, pepper and bay leaf in the water for 1 hour. During the last 10 minutes add the bouillon cubes. Discard the bay leaf. Remove the chicken. Discard the skin and bones and cut the meat into small pieces. Return the chicken pieces to the soup. Add the noodles and simmer for 5 minutes. Heat the butter and sauté the onion and mushrooms for 3 minutes. Add to the soup. Season with salt and pepper and add the sherry, lemon juice and thyme. Simmer for 3 minutes and serve immediately.

Chinese Crabmeat Soup

2 tablespoons oil
1 onion, finely chopped
1 clove garlic, finely chopped
2 tablespoons flour
7 ounce can crabmeat
4 cups chicken stock
2 tablespoons dry sherry
1 tablespoon soy sauce
2 tablespoons finely chopped parsley

Heat the oil and sauté the onion and garlic for 3 minutes. Stir in the flour. Add the remaining ingredients and simmer gently for 3 minutes until the soup is hot.

Thai Rice Soup with Fish

1 cup uncooked rice
6 cups fish stock
4 tablespoons oil
10 cloves garlic, finely chopped
¾ pound fresh fish fillets, cut into bite sized pieces
2 tablespoons soy sauce
4 tablespoons finely chopped parsley
4 slices firm white bread, crusts removed and cut into croutons

This soup should be served in four separate dishes; one holds the soup itself, one contains the sautéed garlic, the third contains the parsley and the fourth holds the croutons. This allows each diner to select his own garnish.
Boil the rice until tender. Drain and stir into the fish stock. Simmer for 15 minutes until the rice disintegrates and thickens the stock. Heat the oil and sauté the garlic in 1 tablespoon of the oil for 3 minutes until lightly browned. Add the fish to the rice broth and add the soy sauce. Simmer for 6 minutes until the fish is white and opaque. Meanwhile fry the diced bread in the remaining oil until crisp and lightly browned. Pour the soup into hot soup bowls.

Japanese Creamed Chicken and Vegetable Soup

Japanese Creamed Chicken and Vegetable Soup

¼ pound bacon, diced
2 tablespoons oil
2 carrots, sliced thinly
2 potatoes, diced
2 onions, finely chopped
1 tablespoon curry powder
6 cups chicken stock
1 clove garlic, peeled
1 teaspoon cornstarch dissolved in 2 teaspoons cold water

Fry the bacon until the fat has rendered and leave to one side. Heat the oil and sauté the carrots, potatoes, onions and curry powder. Cover and cook over low heat for 10 minutes. Add the chicken stock and garlic. Add the bacon and simmer gently for 15 minutes. Discard the garlic. Stir in the cornstarch dissolved in cold water and cook for 2 minutes until the soup has thickened slightly.

Japanese Clear Soup with Poached Egg Triangles

4 5″ squares parchment paper
4 eggs
6 cups chicken stock
1 cup spinach, chopped
1 teaspoon soy sauce
1 strip lemon peel, finely chopped

Half fill a deep saucepan with water and bring to simmering point. Roll each square of parchment paper into a cone and secure with a paper clip. Break an egg into each cone. Lower the cones into the simmering water, folding the edges over the sides of the pan to prevent slippage. Poach the eggs for 6 minutes until cooked. Set in cold water until cool. Slip the eggs from the paper. They will have a triangular shape. Bring the chicken stock to boiling point and add the spinach, soy sauce and lemon peel. Simmer for 5 minutes. Place an egg in each soup bowl and add the hot soup.

80

New Zealand, Australia and Indonesia

Australia and New Zealand do not have an established culinary tradition, rather, their food is reminiscent and reflective of their British heritage. However there are a few soups that are unique to these countries. One of these, a soup that is particularly popular in New Zealand, is called Toheroa, and is a blend of local green mussels, butter, milk and seasonings. Both Australia and New Zealand are famous for their mutton and lambs and many soups are made from these meats. Indonesia is of course famous for a wide range of soups and for its rijsttafel, (literally 'rice table'). One of the many dishes that make up this sumptuous spread is 'sajoer', a clear soup served with vegetables and occasionally garnished with meat. Most Indonesian soups are of European origin, but in recent years a highly spiced broth called 'sope' or 'soto' has become very popular and is of undeniable Indonesian origin.

Above: Cauliflower and Shrimp Soup
Below: New Zealand Cucumber Soup

New Zealand Cucumber Soup

large or 2 small cucumbers, peeled, seeded and sliced
1 onion, thinly sliced
3 tablespoons butter
4 cups chicken stock
5 spinach leaves, chopped
2 cups milk
1 tablespoon cornstarch, dissolved in 2 tablespoons cold water
2 tablespoons chopped chives

Set aside a few cucumber slices for garnishing. Sauté the onion in the butter and add the chicken stock, spinach and remaining cucumber. Simmer for 5 minutes. Rub the soup through a strainer or purée in an electric blender. Return to the saucepan and add the milk. Heat to simmering point and stir in the cornstarch dissolved in cold water. Heat for 2 minutes and garnish with chopped chives and reserved cucumber slices.

Indonesian Fish Soup with Ketchup
Piendang Ketjap

4 cups water
1 onion, finely chopped
1 clove garlic, finely chopped
½ teaspoon sambal oelek
2 daun salam leaves or
2 bay leaves
1 stick sereh
1 teaspoon laos
2 tablespoons ketchup
1 tablespoon lemon juice
¼ pound fish fillets cut into bite sized pieces
¼ pound shrimp, shelled, deveined and cut into small pieces
½ cup bean sprouts

The Indonesian herbs and spices in this recipe can be found in stores specializing in Indonesian and Oriental foods.
Bring the water to the boil and add all the ingredients except the fish pieces, shrimp and bean sprouts. Simmer gently for 15 minutes. Discard the daun salam or bay leaves and the sereh stick. Add the remaining ingredients and simmer for 2 minutes. Serve immediately.

New Zealand Mussel and Spinach Soup
Toheroa

3 quarts fresh mussels
3 sprigs parsley
½ cup chopped celery tops
1 onion, finely chopped
1 tablespoon butter
freshly ground black pepper
4 tablespoons butter
3 tablespoons flour
4 cups milk
¼ pound spinach, heavy stems removed and chopped
1 teaspoons salt
1 tablespoon paprika

New Zealand has a special native green mussel that imparts its color to the soup. Assuming that these are unavailable, spinach has been added to this recipe to provide color.
Wash the mussels well under running water and remove the beards. Discard any that are open. Put the mussels into a large saucepan and add the parsley, celery tops, onion, butter and pepper. Cover and cook over medium heat, shaking the pan from time to distribute the liquid from the mussels evenly. When the mussels have opened, strain the liquid through several thicknesses of cheesecloth and reserve. Remove the mussels from the shells and chop them finely. Heat the remaining butter and stir in the flour. Add the reserved mussel liquid and the milk gradually. Add the spinach and chopped mussels. Simmer for 3 minutes. Season with salt and ladle into soup bowls. Sprinkle the soup with paprika.

Madura Soup
Soto Madura

2 tablespoons oil
2 cloves garlic, finely chopped
2 small onions, finely chopped
1 stick sereh
5 djeruk purut
5 cups chicken stock
1 slice ginger root
1 teaspoon salt
½ cup bean sprouts
1 ounce socen
2 hard-boiled eggs, sliced
2 tablespoons celery tops, finely chopped
1 tablespoon dehydrated onion
½ cup cooked chicken, diced

The ginger root and other special spices essential to the preparation of this delightful soup are available in shops specializing in Indonesian and Oriental foods.
Heat the oil and sauté the garlic and onions for 3 minutes until golden brown. Add the sereh and djeruk purut and sauté for 1 minute. Add the chicken stock and ginger root and simmer for 15 minutes. Season with salt. Discard the sereh and ginger root. Add the bean sprouts and socen and cook for 1 minute. Divide the sliced egg, celery tops, dried onions and chicken between 4 bowls and add the hot soup.

Cauliflower and Shrimp Soup

2 tablespoons oil
2 onions, finely chopped
1 clove garlic, finely chopped
½ teaspoon sambal oelek
½ teaspoon ground ginger
4 cups water
2 chicken bouillon cubes
1 pound cauliflower flowerets
¼ pound shrimp, shelled and deveined

Heat the oil and sauté the onions, garlic, sambal oelek and ginger for 3 minutes. Stir in the water and bouillon cubes and add the cauliflower. Simmer for 15 minutes. Add the shrimp and cook for 3 minutes.

North America

In America, soup and sandwiches are very often served at lunch time and in recent years there has been a significant trend towards the homemade rather than the canned soups. The most popular soup is the New England clam chowder that had its origin with the Breton fishermen. It was traditional in France for part of every catch to be donated to the local fishing village. The fish, together with vegetables, potatoes and herbs were put into an enormous cauldron called a 'chaudière'. When the French fishermen settled in the New World they carried their traditions with them and gradually their soup came to be known as 'chowder'.

New England Clam Chowder

1 quart soft shell, steamer clams
or 2 (8 ounce) cans minced clams
3 small potatoes, peeled and diced
3 slices bacon, cut into small pieces
1 medium sized onion, finely chopped
3 cups milk
1 cup heavy cream
1 tablespoon butter
½ teaspoon salt
freshly ground black pepper

Scrub the clams in cold running water. Place in a large saucepan with ½ cup water. Cover and steam for 8 minutes until the shells open. Discard the shells. Remove the clams and chop them finely. Strain the clam juice through several thicknesses of cheesecloth. Boil the potatoes in salted water for 15 minutes. Fry the bacon in a saucepan until the fat has rendered. Remove the bacon and fry the onion in 1 tablespoon of the bacon fat. Add the strained clam juice or broth from canned clams. Simmer for 5 minutes. Add the chopped clams, milk, cream, butter and potatoes. Simmer for 5 minutes. Garnish bowls with freshly ground black pepper and bacon.

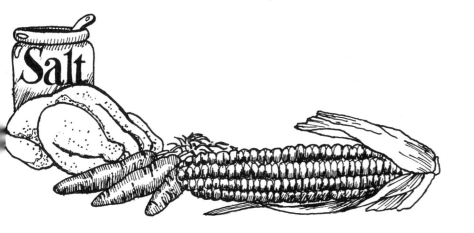

Pennsylvania Corn and Chicken Soup

3 pound chicken cut into serving pieces
5 cups water
1 teaspoon salt
8 peppercorns
1 onion, chopped
2 carrots, sliced
3 chicken bouillon cubes
3 cups canned corn
2 hard-boiled eggs, finely chopped
2 tablespoons finely chopped parsley

Place the chicken in a large saucepan and add the water, salt, peppercorns, onion and carrots. Bring to boiling point. Reduce the heat to simmer. Cover and cook for 1½ hours until the chicken is tender. Remove the chicken from the pan. Discard the skin and bones and cut the meat into small pieces. Return the meat to the pan. Add the bouillon cubes and corn and heat for 5 minutes. Serve the soup garnished with chopped eggs and parsley.

Cold Tomato Soup

3 cups tomato juice
2 tablespoons tomato paste
4 scallions, finely chopped
1 tablespoon fresh thyme leaves or 1 teaspoon dried thyme
⅛ teaspoon cayenne pepper
1 teaspoon salt
1 teaspoon sugar
grated rind of ½ lemon
1 tablespoon lemon juice
½ cup sour cream
2 tablespoons finely chopped parsley

Combine all the ingredients except the sour cream and parsley. Stir well. Cover and chill for 2 hours. Top each serving with a spoonful of sour cream and garnish with parsley.

Creole Soup

Avocado Soup

3 tablespoons butter
3 tablespoons flour
2 cups milk
2 cups chicken stock
1 teaspoon salt
freshly ground black pepper
¼ teaspoon ginger powder
grated rind 1 orange
2 ripe avocadoes
½ cup heavy cream, stiffly whipped
paprika

This soup can be served either hot or cold. Heat the butter, stir in the flour and add the milk and chicken stock gradually. Season with salt, pepper and ginger powder. Add the grated orange rind and simmer for 10 minutes. Peel the avocadoes and mash one. Cut the other into small pieces and reserve for garnish. Stir the mashed avocado into the soup. If the soup is to be served cold, cover tightly with transparent wrap to prevent discoloration. Chill for 4 hours. Spoon in the reserved chopped avocado. Top with whipped cream and sprinkle with paprika.

Avocado Soup

Creole Soup

2 tablespoons peanut oil
1 onion, finely chopped
1 tablespoon flour
2 cups milk
1 teaspoon salt
½ teaspoon celery salt
½ cup peanut butter
2 cups tomato juice
1 medium sized tomato, peeled seeded and chopped
2 tablespoons finely chopped unsalted roasted peanuts

Heat the oil and sauté the onion for 3 minutes. Stir in the flour and add the milk gradually. Add the salt and celery salt. Stir in the peanut butter and simmer for 10 minutes. Add the tomato juice and simmer for 5 minutes. Garnish the soup with the chopped tomato and peanuts.

Canadian Pea Soup

1 pound lean pork loin
2 tablespoons prepared mustard
1 pound green or yellow split peas
8 cups water
1 onion, finely chopped
1 turnip, diced
1 carrot, diced
1 teaspoon summer savory
1 clove garlic, finely chopped
½ teaspoon dried mint
1 teaspoon salt
freshly ground black pepper
1 cup beer
2 tablespoons finely chopped parsley

Rub the mustard into the pork and refrigerate overnight. Soak the split peas in the water overnight. Place the pork, split peas, onion, turnip, carrot, summer savory, garlic, mint, salt and pepper in a large saucepan. Cover and simmer over low heat for 2 hours until the pork is tender and the peas are soft. Remove the pork and cut it into small pieces. Purée the soup in an electric blender and return it to the saucepan. Add the pork and beer. Heat until hot and garnish with parsley.

Canadian Cheese Soup

4 tablespoons butter
1 onion, finely chopped
3 tablespoons finely chopped celery tops
3 tablespoons flour
4 cups chicken stock
½ pound Cheddar cheese, grated
2 cups warm milk
2 tablespoons finely chopped parsley or
1 teaspoon chopped fresh chervil

Heat the butter and sauté the onion and celery tops for 5 minutes. Stir in the flour and add the chicken stock gradually. Simmer for 10 minutes. Add the grated cheese, and cook, stirring constantly until the cheese has melted. Do not allow the soup to regain the boil or the cheese will become tough and stringy. Stir in the warm milk and serve garnished with parsley or chervil.

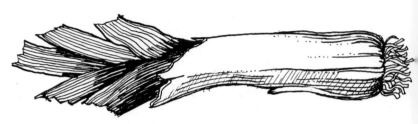

Vichyssoise

2 tablespoons butter
4 leeks, or 4 onions, thinly sliced
4 medium sized potatoes, peeled and diced
6 cups chicken stock
1 cup light cream
1 teaspoon salt
freshly ground black pepper
1 teaspoon chervil
2 tablespoons chopped chives

This cold, creamed soup was created by Louis Diat the head chef of the old Ritz-Carlton Hotel in New York City. The French on the whole do not care for cold soup but vichyssoise is an exception to the rule. Maybe it is because though the soup was created in America, it was a Frenchman who created it and named it after his home town, Vichy. Though the soup is usually served cold, it is equally good hot.

Heat the butter and sauté the leeks or onions for 5 minutes. Add the potatoes and chicken stock. Cover and simmer over low heat for 25 minutes. Rub through a strainer or purée in an electric blender. Stir in the cream and season with salt, pepper and chervil. Chill the soup for 4 hours and garnish with chives.

Cabbage and Ham Soup

4 tablespoons butter
1 green pepper, seeded and chopped
2 stalks celery, sliced
1 onion, finely chopped
3 tablespoons flour
6 cups chicken stock
½ pound boiled ham, diced
1 bay leaf
4 cups cabbage, shredded
2 tablespoons finely chopped parsley
½ cup sour cream

Heat 2 tablespoons of the butter and sauté the pepper, celery and onion for 5 minutes. Stir in the flour and add the chicken stock gradually. Add the ham and bay leaf. Cover and simmer for 20 minutes. In the meantime, heat the remaining butter and sauté the shredded cabbage for 5 minutes. Add ½ cup water. Cover and steam over low heat for 10 minutes. The cabbage should still be quite crisp at this time. Stir the cabbage into the soup and add the parsley. Simmer for another 5 minutes. Serve each bowl garnished with a spoonful of sour cream.

Boston Mushroom Soup

2½ cups mushrooms, finely
chopped and 4 mushrooms
thinly sliced
2 cups water
1 teaspoon salt
freshly ground black pepper
½ teaspoon thyme
½ teaspoon Tabasco sauce
3 tablespoons butter
2 tablespoons flour
2 cups warm milk
½ cup light cream
2 tablespoons dry sherry

Reserve the 4 sliced mushrooms for garnish. Simmer the chopped mushrooms in the water for 5 minutes. Add the salt, pepper, thyme and Tabasco sauce. Heat the butter and sauté the sliced mushrooms. Set aside. Stir the flour into the same butter and add the milk gradually. Pour the mixture into the hot soup. Stir in the cream and sherry and garnish with the sliced sautéed mushrooms.

Lake St. John's Bean Soup

4 cups water
1 pound fresh lima beans
1 teaspoon salt
½ teaspoon sugar
1 tablespoon finely chopped
summer savory
½ pound bacon, diced
2 small onions, finely chopped
1 cup milk

Bring the water to the boil. Add the beans, salt, sugar and summer savory. Cover and simmer gently for 30 minutes until the beans are soft and tender. Meanwhile fry the bacon until crisp. Sauté the onions in the bacon fat for 5 minutes. Stir the bacon and onions into the soup. Add the milk and simmer until hot.

Cioppino

2 dozen steamer or small
clams
½ cup dried Italian mushrooms
⅓ cup olive oil
2 onions, finely chopped
2 cloves garlic, finely chopped
1 green pepper, seeded and
chopped
4 medium sized tomatoes,
peeled, seeded and chopped
2 cups red wine
1½ teaspoons salt
freshly ground black pepper
1 teaspoon oregano
2 tablespoons tomato paste
1½ pound lobster, cut into
small pieces
1 pound jumbo shrimp, shelled
and deveined
2 pounds striped bass, filleted
and cut into
2″ pieces

Scrub the clams under cold running water. Place in a large saucepan. Add 1 cup of water. Cover and steam over low heat until the shells open. Strain the clams through several layers of cheesecloth and reserve. Set aside the clams in their shells. Soak the dried mushrooms in water for 30 minutes. Heat the olive oil in a large saucepan. Add the onions, garlic, green pepper and drained mushrooms and sauté over medium heat for 5 minutes. Add the tomatoes, red wine, reserved clam broth, salt, pepper, oregano and tomato paste. Cover and simmer for 30 minutes. Add the lobster and cook for 5 minutes. Add the shrimp and striped bass and cook for 5 more minutes. Add the clams and cook for 3 minutes until hot. Serve immediately.

Latin America

Argentina's national dish is a thick soup by the name of puchero, and has much in common with the Spanish cocido. Puchero is also popular in Columbia and Bolivia, countries whose cooking reflect the influence of the Spanish and Portuguese settlers who came to Latin America in search of gold. Many remained in their adopted country and intermarried with the native Indian population: thus the two cuisines became intermingled. The result is what we know today and the typical cooking of South America. Olive oil, onions, and green peppers are used throughout South America. Venezuela has few if any regional specialties. Her cuisine is largely influenced by France. The Mexicans, on the other hand have a style of cooking that is uniquely her own and makes use of the ingredients found throughout this continent, and in addition, chocolate is used to flavor both soups and sauces.

Brown Bean Soup with Meat and Oranges
Feijoada

1 pound brown beans
10 cups water
1 clove garlic, finely chopped
1 bay leaf
⅛ teaspoon cayenne pepper
peel of 1 orange
1 cup boiled ham, diced
¾ pound bacon, diced
2 onions, finely chopped
2 small oranges, cut into sections
3 tablespoons finely chopped parsley
½ pound corned beef, diced
6 ounce can cocktail sausages
1 teaspoon salt
freshly ground black pepper

This soup, the national dish of Brazil, makes a complete meal. It is often served with a side dish of rice, which may be added to the soup.

Soak the beans overnight in the water. Add the garlic, bay leaf, cayenne pepper, and orange peel. Simmer gently for 1 hour. Stir in the ham, bacon and chopped onions and simmer for 30 minutes more. During the last 10 minutes of cooking add the orange sections, parsley, corned beef and sausages. Discard the bay leaf and orange peel and season with salt and pepper.

Mexican Clear Soup with Meatballs

Mexican Clear Soup with Meatballs
Albóndigas

½ pound ground beef
1 teaspoon salt
2 tablespoons chili sauce
1 small onion, grated
1 slice white bread, trimmed
2 tablespoons cold water
¼ cup chopped Brazil nuts
1 egg, lightly beaten
6 cups chicken stock
2 teaspoons dried mint
¼ teaspoon saffron
¼ cup dry sherry

Combine the ground beef with the salt, 2 tablespoons of chili sauce, onion, bread, water and nuts. Add the egg and stir lightly. Form the mixture into small meatballs. Bring the stock to boiling point and add the mint and saffron. Reduce the heat and add the meatballs. Simmer for minutes until the meatballs rise to the surface. Stir in the sherry.

Avocado and Potato Soup

Avocado and Potato Soup

4 tablespoons butter
3 onions, finely chopped
4 medium sized potatoes, peeled and diced
4 cups chicken stock
¼ teaspoon saffron
3 cups milk
1 cup canned corn
3 eggs
¼ pound cream cheese
2 tablespoons chili sauce
1 teaspoon salt
freshly ground black pepper
2 avocadoes, peeled and thinly sliced
2 tablespoons finely chopped celery tops

Heat the butter and sauté the onions for 3 minutes. Add the potatoes, chicken stock and saffron and bring to boiling point. Cover and simmer for 20 minutes. Mash one of the potatoes into the soup to thicken it slightly. Stir in the milk and corn. Beat the eggs into the cream cheese and stir into the hot soup. Add the remaining chili sauce, salt and pepper. Place a few slices of avocado in each soup plate and ladle in the soup. Garnish with chopped celery tops.

Chilean Pork Soup with Rice

3 tablespoons oil
1 green pepper, seeded and chopped
1 green or red chili pepper, seeded and chopped
1 onion, finely chopped
½ pound pork, cut into thin strips
1 clove garlic, finely chopped
½ cup uncooked rice
16 ounce can Italian plum tomatoes, chopped
4 cups chicken stock
1 cup red wine
½ teaspoon oregano
¼ cup raisins
2 tablespoons almonds, blanched and chopped
1 teaspoon salt

Heat the oil and sauté the pepper and chili pepper for 2 minutes. Add and sauté the onion, pork and garlic for 5 minutes. Stir in the rice and cook for 3 minutes. Add the tomatoes, chicken stock, wine and oregano. Simmer gently for 30 minutes. During the final 10 minutes add the raisins and almonds. Taste and add the salt if necessary.

Mexican Soup with Chocolate

2 tablespoons olive oil
½ green pepper, seeded and chopped
1 onion, finely chopped
1 clove garlic, finely chopped
5 cups chicken stock
3 tablespoons tomato paste
⅛ teaspoon aniseed
1 tablespoon chili sauce
1 teaspoon cinnamon
2 ounces bitter chocolate, grated
1 tablespoon slivered almonds
1 teaspoon salt
freshly ground black pepper

The chocolate in this piquant soup adds an unexpected and delicious flavor. Heat the oil and sauté the pepper, onion and garlic for 5 minutes. Add the remaining ingredients and simmer gently for 30 minutes. Rub the soup through a strainer or purée in an electric blender. Season with salt and pepper.

Brazilian Chicken Curry Soup

2½ pound chicken, cut into serving pieces
1 onion, finely chopped
1 carrot, sliced
2 stalks celery, sliced
4 sprigs parsley
1 bay leaf
1 teaspoon salt
freshly ground black pepper
1 teaspoon rosemary
8 cups water
2 tablespoons flour
3 tablespoons curry powder
2 red or green peppers, seeded and chopped
1 cup cooked warm rice
1 tablespoon butter

Place the chicken in a large saucepan and add the onion, carrot, celery, parsley, bay leaf, salt, pepper, rosemary and water. Cover and simmer for 1 hour until the chicken is tender. Remove the chicken. Discard the skin and bones and cut the meat into small pieces. Strain the soup. Combine the flour and curry powder and blend in ½ cup of the stock. Pour this mixture back into the soup stirring constantly. Add the peppers. Add the chicken meat and simmer for 10 minutes. Butter 6 small containers and pack with the cooked rice pressing down firmly. Invert the container into the soup bowls and release the rice in a mound. Cover with hot soup.

Brazilian Chicken and Rice Soup

2 tablespoons olive oil
2 (2½ pound) chickens, cut into serving pieces
2 onions, finely chopped
1 clove garlic, finely chopped
8 cups boiling water
4 chicken bouillon cubes
1 small can tomato paste
1 bay leaf
4 sprigs parsley
1 teaspoon marjoram
1 teaspoon salt
freshly ground black pepper
1 tablespoon paprika
½ cup uncooked rice
½ cup boiled ham, diced
2 tablespoons finely chopped parsley

Heat the oil and brown the chicken on all sides. Add the onions and garlic and sauté for 3 minutes. Add the boiling water, bouillon cubes, tomato paste, bay leaf, parsley and marjoram and simmer for 1 hour. Add the salt, pepper and paprika. Add the rice. Bring back to the boil and simmer for another 20 minutes. Remove the chicken from the soup and discard the skin and bones. Cut the meat into small pieces and return the meat to the pan. Discard the bay leaf and parsley and add the diced ham. Heat until hot and garnish with parsley.

South American Bean Soup

1 pound mixed dried legumes, e.g. white and brown beans, chick peas, split peas, lentils etc.
10 cups water
2 bay leaves
2 soup bones
1 whole onion
3 onions, finely chopped
1 clove garlic, finely chopped
3 tablespoons oil
1 pound Polish sausage
2 tablespoons chili sauce
½ teaspoon Tabasco sauce
1 tablespoon paprika
2 tablespoons finely chopped parsley

This soup makes an excellent first course. Soak the legumes overnight in the water. Bring to simmering point and add the bay leaves, soup bones and whole onion. Simmer gently for 2 hours until all the beans and peas are tender. Discard the bay leaves and soup bones and rub all but 2 cups of the soup through a strainer or purée in an electric blender. Sauté the chopped onions and garlic for 10 minutes in the oil. Add the sausage and brown on all sides. Add to the puréed soup. Add the 2 cups of the reserved soup, chili sauce, Tabasco sauce and paprika. Simmer gently for 20 minutes. Garnish with the parsley and serve with French bread.

Argentinian Puchero

¼ pound yellow split peas or chick peas
1 pound lean beef
2 cloves garlic, finely chopped
1 teaspoon salt
freshly ground black pepper
½ teaspoon prepared mustard
½ cup bacon, diced
10 cups water
5 cups cabbage, shredded
2 onions, finely chopped
1 Polish sausage weighing approximately 1 pound
2 potatoes, peeled and diced
2 leeks or 1 onion, sliced
1 cucumber, diced
1 small can tomato paste
½ cup red wine
1 teaspoon salt
freshly ground black pepper

This soup, which originated in Spain, can be found all over South America.
Soak the peas overnight in just enough water to cover. Place the beef, garlic, salt, pepper and mustard in a large saucepan and leave to marinate for 30 minutes. Add the bacon, 10 cups of water and bring to boiling point. Cover and simmer for 1 hour. Drain the peas and add them to the soup together with the cabbage and onions. Simmer for 30 minutes. Add the sausage, potatoes, leeks and cucumber and simmer for another 15 minutes. If the soup is too thick add a little more water. Add the tomato paste and wine. Season with salt and pepper.
Remove the sausage from the soup and cut into thick slices. With a slotted spoon remove the vegetables and meat and arrange on a platter with the sliced sausage. Ladle the soup into bowls and serve with the meat and vegetables. French bread makes an ideal accompaniment to this soup.

South American Potato Soup

3 medium sized potatoes, peeled and diced
5 cups chicken stock
½ teaspoon marjoram
½ teaspoon rosemary
1 green pepper, seeded and chopped
1 onion, finely chopped
2 tablespoons olive oil
¼ pound salami
¼ pound spinach, chopped

Boil the potatoes for 20 minutes in the chicken stock. Add the marjoram and rosemary. Sauté the pepper and onion in the oil until golden brown and add to the soup together with the salami and spinach. Simmer for 10 more minutes.

Argentinian Vegetable Soup

¼ pound yellow split peas
6 cups water
4 chicken bouillon cubes
1 medium sized eggplant, diced
1 large potato, peeled and diced
1½ cups canned corn
½ cucumber, peeled and diced
⅛ teaspoon cayenne pepper
½ teaspoon salt
freshly ground black pepper

Soak the peas overnight in the water. Add the bouillon cubes and simmer for 1 hour. Stir in the remaining ingredients. Season with salt and pepper and simmer for another 30 minutes until the vegetables are tender.

Peruvian Shrimp and Mussel Soup

2 tablespoons butter
2 onions, finely chopped
2 cups fish stock
2 cups dry white wine
freshly ground black pepper
2 slices day old bread, crusts removed
¼ cup milk
¼ pound shrimp, cooked and shelled
1 quart mussels, cooked
⅛ teaspoon cayenne pepper
2 tablespoons ground almonds
1 teaspoon paprika
1 hard-boiled egg, finely chopped
1 teaspoon salt

Heat the butter and sauté the onions for 3 minutes. Stir in the fish stock and wine and season with pepper. Simmer for 30 minutes. Soak the bread in the milk, squeeze out the excess moisture and use a fork to break the bread into small pieces. Stir into the soup. Slice the shrimp and mussels diagonally and add to the soup. Add the cayenne pepper, almonds, paprika and hard-boiled egg. Heat until hot and add the salt.

Tunisian Fish Soup

South African Cold Parsley Soup

1 bunch parsley, approximately
1 cup chopped
4 cups chicken stock
2 egg yolks
1 cup light cream
1 teaspoon salt
freshly ground black pepper
⅛ teaspoon cayenne pepper
6 sprigs parsley

Simmer the parsley in the stock for 20 minutes. Purée in an electric blender and return to the heat. Stir the egg yolks with the cream and add a few spoonfuls of the hot soup. Stir this mixture into the hot soup and heat until hot but do not allow to boil. Season with salt and pepper. Add the cayenne pepper. Cool the soup, cover and refrigerate for 4 hours. Serve in small bowls and garnish with sprigs of parsley.

Africa

Soup is an important part of the diet throughout Africa in the rich and poor regions alike. In the poorer countries, the main meal often consists of a soup based on fish or chicken and prepared with palm oil, chili peppers, okra, tomatoes, onions, ginger and peanuts. The African cuisine is not widely known beyond its boundaries but it has itself been influenced both by Europe and Asia. Africa has an abundance of fruits including oranges, bananas, mangoes, water melons, pineapples and coconuts, all of which contribute an important part to her cooking.

Tunisian Fish Soup

2 tablespoons oil
2 onions, finely chopped
3 cloves garlic, finely chopped
2 teaspoons paprika
1 teaspoon curry powder
4 medium sized ripe tomatoes, peeled, seeded and chopped
4 cups water
2 chicken bouillon cubes
1 pound fish fillets, e.g. cod, haddock, etc. cut into bite sized pieces
1 teaspoon salt
freshly ground black pepper

Heat the oil and sauté the onions and garlic for 10 minutes over low heat. Add the paprika and curry powder. Stir in the tomatoes and add the water and bouillon cubes. Bring the soup to the boil. Reduce to simmering point. Add the fish and cook for 6 minutes until white and opaque. Add the salt and pepper.

Senegalese Cold Soup

3 tablespoons butter
1 onion, finely chopped
2 leeks, finely chopped
1 tablespoon curry powder
2 tablespoons flour
2 teaspoons powdered ginger
5 cups chicken stock
1 small apple, peeled, cored and grated
½ cup cooked chicken, finely chopped
½ cup light cream
1 teaspoon salt
freshly ground black pepper

Heat the butter and sauté the onion and leeks with the curry powder for 3 minutes. Stir in the flour and ginger. Add the stock gradually. Add the apple. Simmer the soup for 30 minutes and purée in an electric blender. Add the chicken and cream. Chill in the refrigerator for 4 hours. Taste and season with salt and pepper if necessary.

West African Peanut Soup

½ pound unsalted, shelled, roasted peanuts, ground
1 onion, finely chopped
4 cups chicken stock
1 tablespoon cornstarch
1 cup light cream
1 teaspoon salt
freshly ground black pepper
⅛ teaspoon cayenne pepper
2 teaspoons paprika
1 tablespoon finely chopped parsley or chives

Nearly every West African country has its own special peanut soup. This rich version tastes even better if it is made a day in advance.
Cook the peanuts and onion gently in the stock for 1 hour. Purée in an electric blender. Stir the cornstarch into the cream and add to the puréed soup. Season with salt and pepper. Add the cayenne pepper and paprika and simmer for 10 minutes. Garnish with parsley or chives.

Nigerian Chicken Soup

2½ pound chicken cut into serving pieces
juice 1 lemon
1 tablespoon paprika
5 cups water
1 teaspoon salt
1 green pepper, seeded and chopped
1 onion, finely chopped
1 small can tomato paste
freshly ground black pepper
2 tomatoes, peeled, seeded and chopped

Rub the chicken pieces with the lemon juice and paprika and add half of the water and salt. Cover and simmer for 30 minutes. Add the remaining water and all the remaining ingredients. Continue cooking for 30 minutes. Remove the chicken. Discard the skin and bones and cut the meat into small pieces. Return the meat to the pan and simmer for 10 minutes.

Ghanian Eggplant and Crabmeat Soup

4 tablespoons oil
6 small onions, finely chopped
1 green pepper, seeded and chopped
1 medium sized eggplant, chopped
8 cups chicken stock
4 large tomatoes, peeled, seeded and chopped
7 ounce can crabmeat
1 teaspoon salt
freshly ground black pepper

Heat the oil and sauté the onions, green pepper and eggplant for 5 minutes. Rub through a strainer or purée in an electric blender. Bring the stock to the boil and add the tomatoes. Simmer for 30 minutes until the vegetables are soft. Rub through a strainer or purée in an electric blender. Break up the crabmeat with a fork. Discard any bones and cartilage and add to the soup. Season with salt and pepper and simmer for 15 minutes.

Coconut Soup

5 cups chicken stock
½ cup shredded coconut
1 tablespoon uncooked rice
1 small eggplant, peeled and chopped
1 tablespoon vinegar or lemon juice
½ teaspoon salt
½ teaspoon ground ginger
2 tablespoons finely chopped parsley

Bring the stock to boiling point. Add the coconut, rice, eggplant, vinegar or lemon juice. Simmer for 35 minutes. Rub the soup through a strainer or purée in an electric blender. Season with salt and ginger and garnish with parsley.

Cooking Terms

Au bain marie The French term for preparing or heating ingredients in a pan, bowl or dish over hot water. In this way the pan containing the ingredients does not come in direct contact with the source of heat.

Bisque The French term for a thickened soup containing shellfish.

Bouilli-meat The French term for a large piece of beef used for preparing a stock.

Bouquet Garni The French term for various herbs, bound together or tied up in a piece of muslin, used when preparing soup or stock. They are removed before serving. The most common herbs are thyme, parsley and bay leaves. Commercially prepared dried bouquet garnis are also available.

Bread Croutons Pieces of day-old bread, without crust, cut into certain shapes and fried in butter or fat. They can be used as a garnish in the soup or served separately as an accompaniment.

Clarify To clear a stock by adding two egg whites and two washed, broken egg shells to a cold, fat-free stock. The stock is then brought to the boil, whisking continuously and after 15 minutes cooling time, strained through a piece of wet cheese cloth placed over a sieve.

Julienne The French term for small strips of vegetables, meat, fish or poultry used as a garnish for soups.

Roux Sauce A basic sauce of flour and butter, mixed with stock or water.

Sauté To fry vegetables and/or herbs, gently in butter, oil or fat in an open pan.

Skim To remove scum from a stock so that it becomes clear.

Soup Meat Small scraps of veal, lamb or beef, unfit for roasting or braising but ideal for making a stock.

Garnishes for Clear Soups

A simple cup of clear soup made with a commercial stock preparation can be made to look far more attractive if it is garnished with a slice of lemon, chopped garden herbs or finely chopped red pepper for example.

One must be very careful in choosing the garnish for a clear soup however. A delicious aromatic, home-made clear soup needs very little garnish, in fact it only needs a visual garnish. A clear soup made from a commercial stock preparation can be given that extra little bit of flavor by adding one of the following garnish suggestions:

wafer thin slices of lemon or orange;
finely chopped fresh herbs, chervil, celery greens, parsley, mint, chives, thyme or marjoram;
dried herbs, soaked for an hour in water before using, – such as thyme, mint or marjoram;
finely chopped onion, mushrooms, peeled and de-seeded tomatoes, hard-boiled egg yolk;
cooked rice, vermicelli, fancy macaroni;
peeled grapes;
finely sliced omelette;
poached eggs; (see recipe on the right)
fishballs; (see recipe on the right)
dumplings; (see recipe on the right)
crispy fried, crumbled bacon;
crumbled potato crisps;

Useful Soup Accompaniments are:

breadsticks;
melba toast;
rusks;
slice of lemon;
grated cheese;
warm cooked rice;
bread croutons;
unsweetened heavy cream;
sour cream;
French bread, fresh or warmed in the oven, wrapped in aluminium foil on the barbecue, or under a pre-heated grill.

Meatballs

$\frac{1}{4}$ pound ground veal
1 slice of white bread, without crust, soaked in a little milk
pepper
salt
1 tablespoon finely chopped parsley
pinch of nutmeg, optional
finely chopped onion, optional

Mix the ground veal with the soaked and squeezed out slice of bread, salt and pepper, parsley and nutmeg and onion if wished. Roll into small balls using wet hands and simmer them for about 10 minutes in the stock, until cooked through.

Fishballs

Make in the same way as the meatballs but replace the meat with the same amount of filleted fish. Season with a few drops of lemon juice and use dill or thyme (fresh, dried or powdered) instead of the parsley.

Dumplings

4 tablespoons butter
1 egg
2 cups flour
$\frac{1}{2}$ teaspoon salt
2 tablespoons water

Beat the butter with the egg until creamy and stir in the flour, salt and enough water to make a firm dough. Mould into small balls and poach in the stock for about 10 minutes until they float to the surface.

Poached Eggs

Keep the stock just under the boiling point. Break an egg into a cup and slide it into the stock. Poach gently for 3–4 minutes and remove with a slotted spoon. Always poach eggs one at a time in the stock – place in the soup bowl or plate and pour over the warm stock.

Alphabetical Index

Aargau Spinach Soup 23
Allgäuer Soup with Liver Dumplings 50
Argentinian Puchero 91
Argentinian Vegetable Soup 91
Artichoke Soup 18
Asparagus Soup 46
Austrian Leafy Green Soup 62
Austrian Oatmeal Soup 61
Austrian Sauerkraut Soup 59
Avocado and Potato Soup 89
Avocado Soup 85

Barley Soup 49
Bavarian Beer Soup 52
Bean and Bacon Soup 45
Bean and Tomato Soup 49
Beef and Vegetable Soup 22
Beer Soup 54
Billi-bi 22
Black Soup 55
Borsht with Meat 69
Boston Mushroom Soup 87
Bouillabaisse 19
Bouillon 58
Bouillon with Cheese Dumplings 62
Bouillon with Liver Dumplings 58
Brazilian Chicken and Rice Soup 90
Brazilian Chicken Curry Soup 90
Breton Fish Soup 20
Brown Bean Soup 47
Brown Bean Soup with Meat and Oranges 88
Brussels Sprout Soup 40
Bulgarian Lamb Soup 65
Bulgarian Soup with Dumplings 66

Cabbage and Ham Soup 86
Cabbage Soup – Scandinavia 57
Cabbage Soup – Switzerland 24
Canadian Cheese Soup 86
Canadian Pea Soup 86
Carmen's Chestnut Soup 30
Carnival Soup 51
Cauliflower and Shrimp Soup 82
Chanterelle Soup 61
Cheese Soup 44
Chestnut Soup 28
Chicken and Corn Soup 78
Chicken Soup with Meatballs 49
Chilean Pork Soup with Rice 89
Chinese Crabmeat Soup 79
Chinese Vegetable Soup with Shrimp 78
Chlodnik 62
Chrysanthemum Soup 34
Cioppino 87
Clear Celery Soup 36
Clear Chicken and Vegetable Broth 20
Clear Soup with Chicken Dumplings 78
Clear Soup with Poached Eggs 29
Cock-a-Leekie Soup 35

Coconut Soup 94
Cold Cherry Soup 50
Cold Cucumber Soup 75
Cold Tomato Soup 83
Cold Turkish Yogurt Soup 69
Corsican Tomato Soup 16
Creamed Ham Soup 27
Creamed Crab Soup 35
Cream of Carrot Soup 38
Cream of Celery Soup 26
Cream of Onion Soup 35
Creole Soup 85
Croatian Fish Soup 65

Dahl Soup 74
Danish Apple Soup 55

Eggplant Soup 27

Flemish Buttermilk Soup 43
Flemish Vegetable Hodgepodge 43
Finnish Fish Soup 56
Fish Soup 27
Fish Soup with Pineapple 77
Fruit Soup 56

Garbure Béarnaise 18
Garlic Soup 19
Gazpacho 30
Geneva Potato Soup 23
Genoese Minestrone 28
Ghanian Eggplant and Crabmeat Soup 94
Ghentian Waterzooi Soup 40
Golem's Soup with Dumplings 59
Greek Egg and Lemon Soup 67
Greek Lentil Soup 63
Greek Vegetable Soup 64
Greek White Bean and Tomato Soup 63
Green Soup 41

Hamburg Eel Soup 53
Hare Soup – Great Britain 38
Hare Soup – Holland 47
Hodge Podge 35
Hungarian Calf's Brain Soup 59
Hungarian Goulash Soup 58

Irish Cabbage Soup 34
Indian Curry Soup with Meat Balls 74
Indonesian Fish Soup with Ketchup 82

Japanese Creamed Chicken and Vegetable
  Soup 80
Jura Mountain Soup 24

Kidney Soup 36

Lady Curzon Soup 34
Lake St. John's Bean Soup 87
Leek and Potato Soup – France 17
Leek and Potato Soup – Holland 47
Liver and Bacon Soup 39

Macaroni and Bean Soup 26

Madura Soup 82
Maritata Soup 28
Meatless Borsht 69
Mexican Clear Soup with Meatballs 88
Mexican Soup with Chocolate 90
Mina's Lemon Soup 57
Minestrone Ernesto 29
Mulligatawny Soup – Great Britain 38
Mulligatawny Soup – India 75
Mushroom and Potato Soup 67
Mushroom Soup 49
Mussel Soup 44

New Delhi Soup 73
New England Clam Chowder 83
New Zealand Cucumber Soup 81
New Zealand Mussel and Spinach Soup 82
Nigerian Chicken Soup 94
North German Lentil Soup 51
Norwegian Cold Fish Soup 54

Onion Soup – Belgium 43
Onion Soup – France 22
Ostend Lentil and Mussel Soup 42
Oxtail Soup 36

Parsley and Rice Soup 26
Pea Soup 54
Peking Pork Soup 77
Pennsylvania Corn and Chicken Soup 83
Persian Barley Soup 75
Persian Onion Soup 76
Persian Prune Soup 75
Persian Vegetable Soup 74
Peruvian Shrimp and Mussel Soup 91
Pigeon Soup 24
Polish Beer Soup 62
Polish Borsht 60
Polynesian Chicken Soup with Noodles 79
Pomegranate Soup 74
Portuguese Egg and Tomato Soup 33
Portuguese Fish Soup 31
Portuguese Green Soup 31
Potage Bonne Femme 18
Potato Soup – Belgium 43
Potato Soup – France 16
Potato Soup – Holland 45
Pot au Feu Basquaise 17
Prague Potato Soup 60
Prussian Cabbage Soup 52

Rassolnik 72
Rose Hip Soup 53
Royal Soup 33
Rumanian Chicken Soup 63
Rumanian Soup with Meatballs 66
Russian Beef Tongue and Vegetable Soup 70
Russian Vegetable Soup with Stuffed Cabbage
  Rolls 70
Russian Wine Soup 71

Salsify Soup 51
Sausage Soup 51
Scotch Broth 39

Schi 71
Senegalese Cold Soup 93
Serbian Spinach Soup 67
Shrimp Soup 46
South African Cold Parsley Soup 93
South American Bean Soup 90
South American Potato Soup
Spanish Asparagus and Hazelnut Soup 42
Spanisch Bean Soup 31
Spanish Chick Pea Soup 32
Spanish Egg Soup 30
Spanish Garlic Soup 32
Spanish Vegetable Soup 31
St. Hubert's Soup 44
Stocks 12–15
Stracciatella 29
Strawberry Soup 71
Swedish Bread Soup 55

Tarator 66
Thai Clear Soup with Fishballs 79
Thai Rice Soup with Fish 79
Thick Pea Soup 46
Tomato Soup with Shrimp 56
Transylvanian Peasant Soup 64
Tunisian Fish Soup 93
Turkish Chicken Soup 71
Turkish Lamb Soup with Tomatoes 70
Turkish Mutton Soup 72
Turnip Soup 42

Vegetable Soup Ticino 23
Vegetable Soup with Meatballs 47
Vichyssoise 86
Vietnamese Vegetable Soup with Shrimp 78

Waterzooi 42
West African Peanut Soup 94
Westphalian Buttermilk Soup 50

SOUPS WITH POTATOES

Geneva Potato Soup 23
Leek and Potato Soup 17
Potato Soup – Belgium 43
Potato Soup – France 16
Potato Soup – Holland 45
Prague Potato Soup 60
South American Potato Soup 91

SOUPS WITH VEGETABLES

Aargau Spinach Soup 23
Argentinian Vegetable Soup 91
Artichoke Soup 18
Asparagus Soup 46
Avocado and Potato Soup 89
Avocado Soup 85
Austrian Leafy Green Soup 62
Bean and Tomato Soup 49
Boston Mushroom Soup 87
Brown Bean Soup 47
Brussels Sprout Soup 40
Cabbage Soup 57
Cauliflower and Shrimp Soup 82
Chanterelle Soup 61
Clear Celery Soup 36
Cold Cucumber Soup 75
Cold Tomato Soup 83
Corsican Tomato Soup 16
Cream of Carrot Soup 38
Cream of Celery Soup 26
Cream of Onion Soup 35
Creole Soup 85
Dahl Soup 74
Eggplant Soup 27
Gazpacho 30
Genoese Minestrone 28
Greek Lentil Soup 63
Greek Vegetable Soup 64
Greek White Bean and Tomato Soup 63
Green Soup 41
Hungarian Goulash Soup 58
Irish Cabbage Soup 34
Jura Mountain Soup 24
Leek and Potato Soup 47
Macaroni and Bean Soup 26
Meatless Borsht 69
Minestrone Ernesto 29
Mulligatawny Soup – Great Britain 38
Mulligatawny Soup – India 75
Mushroom and Potato Soup 67
Mushroom Soup 49
New Delhi Soup 73
New Zealand Cucumber Soup 81
Onion Soup – Belgium 43
Onion Soup – France 22
Parsley and Rice Soup 26

Pea Soup 54
Persian Onion Soup 76
Persian Vegetable Soup 74
Polish Borsht 60
Portuguese Green Soup 31
Potage Bonne Femme 18
Russian Vegetable Soup with Stuffed Cabbage
  Rolls 70
Salsify Soup 51
Senegalese Cold Soup 93
Serbian Spinach Soup 67
South African Cold Parsley Soup 93
South American Bean Soup 90
Spanish Asparagus and Hazelnut Soup 32
Spanish Bean Soup 31
Spanisch Garlic Soup 32
Spanish Vegetable Soup 31
Tomato Soup with Shrimp 56
Turnip Soup 42
Vichyssoise 86
Vietnamese Vegetable Soup with Shrimp 78
Vegetable Soup Ticino 23
Vegetable Soup with Meatballs 47

SOUPS WITH VEGETABLES AND MEAT

Argentinian Puchero 91
Austrian Sauerkraut Soup 59
Bean and Bacon Soup 45
Beef and Vegetable Soup 22
Borsht with Meat 69
Brown Bean Soup with Meat and Oranges 88
Bulgarian Lamb Soup 65
Cabbage and Ham Soup 86
Cabbage Soup 24
Canadian Pea Soup 86
Chilean Pork Soup with Rice 89
Clear Chicken and Vegetable Broth 20
Flemish Vegetable Hodgepodge 43
Garbure Béarnaise 18
Hodge Podge 35
Lake St. John's Bean Soup 87
North German Lentil Soup 51
Oxtail Soup 36
Peking Pork Soup 77
Pot au Feu Basquaise 17
Prussian Cabbage Soup 52
Rassolnik 72
Rumanian Soup with Meatballs 66
Russian Beef Tongue and Vegetable Soup 72
Schi 71
Scotch Broth 39
Spanish Chick Pea Soup 32
Thick Pea Soup 46
Transylvanian Peasant Soup 64
Turkish Lamb Soup with Tomatoes 70
Turkish Mutton Soup 72

SOUPS WITH MEAT

Allgäuer Soup with Liver Dumplings 50
Bouillon with Liver Dumplings 58

Creamed Ham Soup 27
Hungarian Calf's Brain Soup 59
Indian Curry Soup with Meat Balls 74
Kidney Soup 36
Liver and Bacon Soup 39
Mexican Clear Soup with Meatballs 88
Sausage Soup 51

SOUPS WITH FISH

Billi-Bi 22
Bouillabaisse 19
Breton Fish Soup 20
Cauliflower and Fish Soup 82
Chinese Crabmeat Soup 79
Chinese Vegetable Soup with Shrimp 78
Cioppino 87
Creamed Crab Soup 35
Croatian Fish Soup 65
Finnish Fish Soup 56
Fish Soup 27
Fish Soup with Pineapple 77
Ghanian Eggplant and Crabmeat Soup 94
Hamburg Eel Soup 53
Indonesian Fish Soup with Ketchup 82
Mussel Soup 44
New England Clam Chowder 83
New Zealand Mussel and Spinach Soup 82
Norwegian Cold Fish Soup 54
Ostend Lentil and Mussel Soup 42
Peruvian Shrimp and Mussel Soup 91
Portuguese Fish Soup 31
Shrimp Soup 46
Thai Clear Soup with Fishballs 79
Thai Rice Soup with Fish 79
Tomato Soup with Shrimp 56
Tunisian Fish Soup 93
Vietnamese Vegetable Soup with Shrimp 78
Waterzooi 42

SOUPS WITH GAME AND FOWL

Black Soup 55
Brazilian Chicken and Rice Soup 90
Brazilian Chicken Curry Soup 90
Chicken and Corn Soup 78
Chicken Soup with Meatballs 49
Clear Soup with Chicken Dumplings 78
Cock-a-Leekie Soup 35
Ghentian Waterzooi Soup 40
Hare Soup – Great Britain 38
Hare Soup – Holland 47
Japanese Creamed Chicken and Vegetable
   Soup 80
Nigerian Chicken Soup 94
Pennsylvania Corn and Chicken Soup 83
Pigeon Soup 24
Polynesian Chicken Soup with Noodles 79
Rumanian Chicken Soup 63
St. Hubert's Soup 44
Turkish Chicken Soup 71

SOUPS WITH CHEESE AND EGGS, YOGURT OR BUTTERMILK

Bouillon 58
Bouillon with Cheese Dumplings 62
Canadian Cheese Soup 86
Cheese Soup 44
Clear Soup with Poached Eggs 29
Cold Turkish Yogurt Soup 69
Flemish Buttermilk Soup 43
Greek Egg and Lemon Soup 67
Maritata Soup 28
Portuguese Egg and Tomato Soup 33
Spanish Egg Soup 30
Westphalian Buttermilk Soup 50

SOUPS WITH RICE AND MACARONI

Barley Soup 49
Chilean Pork Soup with Rice 89
Genoese Minestrone 28
Macaroni and Bean Soup 26
Minestrone Ernesto 29
Parsley and Rice Soup 26
Thai Rice Soup with Fish

SOUPS WITH WINE AND BEER

Bavarian Beer Soup 52
Beer Soup 54
Polish Beer Soup 62
Russian Wine Soup 71

COLD SOUPS

Avocado Soup 85
Chlodnik 62
Cold Cucumber Soup 75
Cold Tomato Soup 83
Cold Turkish Yogurt Soup 69
Gazpacho 30
Norwegian Cold Fish Soup 54
Senegalese Cold Soup 93
South African Cold Parsley Soup 93
Vichyssoise 86
Cold Cucumber Soup 75

SOUPS WITH FRUITS

Cold Cherry Soup 50
Danish Apple Soup 55
Fruit Soup 56
Mina's Lemon Soup 57
Persian Prune Soup 75
Rose Hip Soup 53
Strawberry Soup 71

VARIOUS SOUPS

Austrian Leafy Green Soup 62
Austrian Oatmeal Soup 61
Avocado Soup 85
Barley Soup 49
Black Soup 55
Bulgarian Soup with Dumplings 66
Carmen's Chestnut Soup 30
Carnival Soup 51
Chestnut Soup 28
Chlodnik 62
Chrysanthemum Soup 34
Coconut Soup 94
Garlic Soup 19
Golem's Soup with Dumplings 59
Greek Egg and Lemon Soup 67
Lady Curzon Soup 34
Madura Soup 82
Mexican Soup with Chocolate 90
Persian Barley Soup 75
Pomegranate Soup 74
Royal Soup 33
Stracciatella 29
Swedish Bread Soup 55
Tarator 66
West African Peanut Soup 94